School Reform

Other Books of Related Interest:

Opposing Viewpoints Series

Charter Schools

Education

High School Alternative Programs

At Issue Series

High School Dropouts

Should Junk Food Be Sold in School?

What Is the Future of Higher Education?

Current Controversies Series

Bullying

College Admissions

Gangs

"Congress shall make no law . . . abridging the freedom of speech, or of the press."

First Amendment to the US Constitution

The basic foundation of our democracy is the First Amendment guarantee of freedom of expression. The Opposing Viewpoints series is dedicated to the concept of this basic freedom and the idea that it is more important to practice it than to enshrine it.

School Reform

Noël Merino, Book Editor

GREENHAVEN PRESS
A part of Gale, Cengage Learning

Farmington Hills, Mich • San Francisco • New York • Waterville, Maine
Meriden, Conn • Mason, Ohio • Chicago

Patricia Coryell, *Vice President & Publisher, New Products & GVRL*
Douglas Dentino, *Manager, New Products*
Judy Galens, *Acquisitions Editor*

WCN: 01-100-101

For more information, contact:
Greenhaven Press
27500 Drake Rd.
Farmington Hills, MI 48331-3535
Or you can visit our Internet site at gale.cengage.com

Articles in Greenhaven Press anthologies are often edited for length to meet page requirements. In addition, original titles of these works are changed to clearly present the main thesis and to explicitly indicate the author's opinion. Every effort is made to ensure that Greenhaven Press accurately reflects the original intent of the authors. Every effort has been made to trace the owners of copyrighted material.

LIBRARY OF CONGRESS CATALOGING-IN-PUBLICATION DATA

School reform / Noël Merino, book editor.
pages cm. -- (Opposing viewpoints)
Includes bibliographical references and index.
ISBN 978-0-7377-7286-9 (hardcover) -- ISBN 978-0-7377-7287-6 (pbk.)
1. Educational change--United States. 2. Education--United States--Finance. 3. Educational tests and measurements--United States. 4. Educational evaluation--United States. I. Merino, Noël.
LA217.2.S373 2015
370.973--dc23

2014040406

Printed in the United States of America
1 2 3 4 5 6 7 19 18 17 16 15

Contents

Chapter 3: What Role Should School Choice Play in School Reform?

Chapter 4: Should Curriculum Content in Schools Be Reformed?

Why Consider Opposing Viewpoints?

> *"The only way in which a human being can make some approach to knowing the whole of a subject is by hearing what can be said about it by persons of every variety of opinion and studying all modes in which it can be looked at by every character of mind. No wise man ever acquired his wisdom in any mode but this."*
>
> *John Stuart Mill*

In our media-intensive culture it is not difficult to find differing opinions. Thousands of newspapers and magazines and dozens of radio and television talk shows resound with differing points of view. The difficulty lies in deciding which opinion to agree with and which "experts" seem the most credible. The more inundated we become with differing opinions and claims, the more essential it is to hone critical reading and thinking skills to evaluate these ideas. Opposing Viewpoints books address this problem directly by presenting stimulating debates that can be used to enhance and teach these skills. The varied opinions contained in each book examine many different aspects of a single issue. While examining these conveniently edited opposing views, readers can develop critical thinking skills such as the ability to compare and contrast authors' credibility, facts, argumentation styles, use of persuasive techniques, and other stylistic tools. In short, the Opposing Viewpoints Series is an ideal way to attain the higher-level thinking and reading skills so essential in a culture of diverse and contradictory opinions.

In addition to providing a tool for critical thinking, Opposing Viewpoints books challenge readers to question their own strongly held opinions and assumptions. Most people form their opinions on the basis of upbringing, peer pressure, and personal, cultural, or professional bias. By reading carefully balanced opposing views, readers must directly confront new ideas as well as the opinions of those with whom they disagree. This is not to argue simplistically that everyone who reads opposing views will—or should—change his or her opinion. Instead, the series enhances readers' understanding of their own views by encouraging confrontation with opposing ideas. Careful examination of others' views can lead to the readers' understanding of the logical inconsistencies in their own opinions, perspective on why they hold an opinion, and the consideration of the possibility that their opinion requires further evaluation.

Evaluating Other Opinions

To ensure that this type of examination occurs, Opposing Viewpoints books present all types of opinions. Prominent spokespeople on different sides of each issue as well as well-known professionals from many disciplines challenge the reader. An additional goal of the series is to provide a forum for other, less known, or even unpopular viewpoints. The opinion of an ordinary person who has had to make the decision to cut off life support from a terminally ill relative, for example, may be just as valuable and provide just as much insight as a medical ethicist's professional opinion. The editors have two additional purposes in including these less known views. One, the editors encourage readers to respect others' opinions—even when not enhanced by professional credibility. It is only by reading or listening to and objectively evaluating others' ideas that one can determine whether they are worthy of consideration. Two, the inclusion of such viewpoints encourages the important critical thinking skill of objectively evaluating an author's credentials and bias. This evaluation will illuminate an author's reasons for taking a particular stance on an issue and will aid in readers' evaluation of the author's ideas.

It is our hope that these books will give readers a deeper understanding of the issues debated and an appreciation of the complexity of even seemingly simple issues when good and honest people disagree. This awareness is particularly important in a democratic society such as ours in which people enter into public debate to determine the common good. Those with whom one disagrees should not be regarded as enemies but rather as people whose views deserve careful examination and may shed light on one's own.

Thomas Jefferson once said that "difference of opinion leads to inquiry, and inquiry to truth." Jefferson, a broadly educated man, argued that "if a nation expects to be ignorant and free . . . it expects what never was and never will be." As individuals and as a nation, it is imperative that we consider the opinions of others and examine them with skill and discernment. The Opposing Viewpoints series is intended to help readers achieve this goal.

David L. Bender and Bruno Leone,
Founders

Introduction

> *"Warnings [in 1983's 'A Nation at Risk'] still reverberate today, with 1 in 4 Americans failing to earn a high school degree on time and the U.S. lagging other countries in the percentage of young people who complete college."*
>
> —*Philip Elliott, Associated Press, April 24, 2013*

The development of the public school system in America began in the nineteenth century. Prior to that, the education of children had been the domain of the family, the church, or private entities. In 1837 Massachusetts was the first state to create a board of education, establishing statewide standards. In 1892 the National Education Association established the Committee of Ten, which recommended the standardization of high school curriculum, primarily to ensure that all children had the adequate basic education necessary to attend college, should they choose to do so. The Committee of Ten gave several recommendations on the offering and content of high school classes in Latin, English, mathematics, and the sciences. As the committee's recommendations were only that, no binding nationwide standards were set as a result. Almost a century later, however, the call for nationwide reform of education launched a debate about school reform that continues to this day.

The secretary of education under President Ronald Reagan, Terrel Bell, asked the National Commission on Excellence in Education to examine the quality of education in the United States. In 1983 the commission released its findings in "A Nation at Risk: The Imperative for Educational Reform," giving a dire assessment of the state of education in the United States.

The report said, "If an unfriendly foreign power had attempted to impose on America the mediocre educational performance that exists today, we might well have viewed it as an act of war. As it stands, we have allowed this to happen to ourselves." The report found little to praise about the American education system and made several suggestions for reform. Yet, more than three decades later, the same problems identified in that report continue to be debated today, with little consensus on how to solve them.

The commission made several recommendations about various components of public school education, including recommendations about standards, teacher pay, and funding. The commission recommended adopting "more rigorous and measurable standards" for learning. Today, all states have adopted academic standards, but controversy still abounds regarding the adoption of federal standards and the best way to assess students. It is far from agreed that much progress has occurred regarding student achievement: Standardized test scores among high school students on the National Assessment of Educational Progress (NAEP) dropped by one point in reading and increased by only four points in math since the early 1980s, according to the National Center for Education Statistics (NCES).

The commission also recommended, "Salaries for the teaching profession should be increased and should be professionally competitive, market-sensitive, and performance-based." According to the NCES, when computed in 2012–2013 school year dollars, the average public school teacher's salary in the 1982–1983 school year was $48,781, whereas in the 2012–2013 school year it had risen to $56,383. Whether or not this increase of just over 15 percent is adequate is in dispute, with some claiming that teachers are underpaid but others saying that with their whole benefits package teachers are overpaid. More than thirty years after "A Nation at Risk," there is debate about whether teachers' pay is adequately tied to performance and whether teachers' unions do enough to ensure that pay and tenure are tied to performance. Controversies about teachers continue to be a large part of the school reform debate, with issues of their pay, training, and union membership remaining contentious.

One of the other issues raised in "A Nation at Risk" was that of funding for education. As a result of the Cold War, the commission notes, "we have dismantled essential support systems." It called "upon citizens to provide the financial support necessary to accomplish these purposes. Excellence costs. But in the long run mediocrity costs far more." In 2010 the annual spending per public school student annually in the United States was second only to Switzerland, according to a study by the Organisation for Economic Co-operation and Development (OECD). Yet, on the 2012 OECD Programme for International Student Assessment (PISA), which measures student performance in math in OECD member countries, the United States ranked twenty-seventh out of thirty-four countries.

The aim of providing good education to American children in public schools is one that has been fraught with controversy since public education began in the United States. Efforts to meet student educational needs with policies that appeal to parents, educators, and politicians inevitably have created debate at both the national and local levels, prompting a variety of questions. The questions posed in the chapters within this volume are "What Policies Should Guide School Reform?," "How Should Students, Teachers, and Schools Be Evaluated?," "What Role Should School Choice Play in School Reform?," and "Should Curriculum Content in Schools Be Reformed?" A wide variety of competing answers to these questions are explored in *Opposing Viewpoints: School Reform*.

What Policies Should Guide School Reform?

Chapter Preface

There is widespread agreement in America that there is room for improvement in the education system. Phi Delta Kappa International (PDK) and Gallup have been conducting an annual poll of the public's attitudes toward public schools for forty-five years. In a 2013 poll, when Americans were asked to grade public schools in the nation as a whole, 1 percent gave the schools an A, 18 percent a B, 53 percent a C, 19 percent a D, and 6 percent said the schools fail (3 percent did not answer). Interestingly, when Americans were asked to grade the public schools in their own communities, 13 percent gave the schools an A, 40 percent a B, 29 percent a C, 11 percent a D, and 4 percent said the schools fail (3 percent did not answer).

When polled about the biggest problems in public schools, more than a third of Americans cited lack of financial support as the biggest issue. This issue has been the leading concern among Americans in the annual PDK/Gallup poll since 2002. Other issues of note that have been cited include lack of discipline, overcrowding, lack of parental support, testing requirements and regulations, fighting, difficulty getting good teachers, and use of drugs.

When asked about specific federal school reform programs, Americans lacked knowledge about recent developments. Whereas 97 percent of Americans had heard about the No Child Left Behind Act, which requires states to develop assessments of students in order to measure basic skills, fewer Americans knew of more recent reform measures. Only 43 percent of Americans said they knew about the Race to the Top competition enacted by President Barack Obama that awards funding based on state initiatives to improve education in areas such as teaching and leadership, standards and assessment, and turning around the lowest-achieving schools. Even fewer—only 38 percent—had heard of the Common Core State Standards, an initiative sponsored by the National Governors Association (NGA) and the Council of Chief State School Officers (CCSSO) launched in 2009 that developed consistent educational standards for use across the United States. As of August 2014, forty-three states and the District of Columbia had adopted the Common Core State Standards.

Agreement on the existence of a problem with public education may be the strongest area of consensus. There is a lack of agreement about the problems faced in education and a lack of knowledge about existing education programs. As authors in the following chapter illustrate, without consensus on the problems and solutions, school reform in the United States faces serious hurdles.

Viewpoint 1

> *"The standards were informed by the best in the country, the highest international standards, and evidence and expertise about educational outcomes."*

The Common Core State Standards Are Good for Education

Council of Chief State School Officers

In the following viewpoint, the Council of Chief State School Officers (CCSSO) argues that despite myths to the contrary, the Common Core State Standards Initiative will not reduce education quality, but will actually help support states in developing curricula that effectively prepare students in an internationally competitive manner. CCSSO is a nationwide organization that works to bring together leaders from every state to address major educational issues.

As you read, consider the following questions:

1. In what way does the author assert that the Common Core State Standards are internationally benchmarked?

Council of Chief State School Officers (CCSSO), "Myths vs. Facts," Common Core State Standards Initiative, 2015. http://www.corestandards.org.

2. What four elements were included in the evidence base used to develop the Common Core State Standards, according to the author?

3. Who decides the means of assessing students in their implementation of the Common Core State Standards, according to the author?

Successful implementation of the Common Core State Standards [Initiative] requires parents, educators, policy makers, and other stakeholders to have the facts about what the standards are and what they are not. The following myths and facts aim to address common misconceptions about the development, intent, content, and implementation of the standards.

The Myths About Content and Quality

Myth: Adopting common standards means bringing all states' standards down to the lowest common denominator. This means that states with high standards are actually taking a step backwards by adopting the Common Core.

Fact: The standards are designed to build upon the most advanced current thinking about preparing all students for success in college, career, and life. This will result in moving even the best state standards to the next level. In fact, since this work began, there has been an explicit agreement that no state would lower its standards. The standards were informed by the best in the country, the highest international standards, and evidence and expertise about educational outcomes. We need college- and career-ready standards because even in high-performing states, students are graduating and passing all the required tests but still need remediation in their postsecondary work.

Myth: The Common Core State Standards are not internationally benchmarked.

Fact: Standards from top-performing countries played a significant role in the development of the math and English language arts/literacy standards. In fact, the college- and career-ready standards provide an appendix listing the evidence that was consulted in drafting the standards, including the international standards that were consulted in the development process.

Myth: The standards only include skills and do not address the importance of content knowledge.

Fact: The standards recognize that both content and skills are important.

The English language arts standards require certain critical content for all students, including classic myths and stories from around the world, America's founding documents, foundational American literature, and [William] Shakespeare. Appropriately, the remaining crucial decisions about what content should be taught are made at the state and local levels. In addition to content coverage, the standards require that students systematically acquire knowledge in literature and other disciplines through reading, writing, speaking, and listening.

The mathematics standards lay a solid foundation in whole numbers, addition, subtraction, multiplication, division, fractions, and decimals. Taken together, these elements support a student's ability to learn and apply more demanding math concepts and procedures. The middle school and high school standards call on students to practice applying mathematical ways of thinking to real-world issues and challenges. They prepare students to think and reason mathematically. The standards set a rigorous definition of college and career readiness not by piling topic upon topic, but by demanding that students develop a depth of understanding and ability to apply mathematics to novel situations, as college students and employees regularly do.

The Myths About Math Standards

Myth: The standards do not prepare or require students to learn algebra in the 8th grade, as many states' current standards do.

Fact: The standards do accommodate and prepare students for Algebra 1 in 8th grade by including the prerequisites for this course in grades K–7. Students who master the K–7 material will be able to take Algebra 1 in 8th grade. At the same time, grade 8 standards also include rigorous algebra and will transition students effectively into a full Algebra 1 course.

Myth: Key math topics are missing or appear in the wrong grade.

Fact: The mathematical progressions presented in the Common Core State Standards are coherent and based on evidence.

Part of the problem with having different sets of state standards in mathematics is that different states cover different topics at different grade levels. Coming to a consensus guarantees that, from the viewpoint of any given state, topics will move up or down in the grade-level sequence. What is important to keep in mind is that the progression in the Common Core State Standards is mathematically coherent and leads to college and career readiness at an internationally competitive level.

The Myths About English Language Arts (ELA) Standards

Myth: The standards are just vague descriptions of skills and do not include a reading list or any other reference to content.

Fact: The standards do include sample texts that demonstrate the level of text complexity appropriate for the grade level and compatible with the learning demands set out in the standards. The exemplars of high-quality texts at each grade level provide a rich set of possibilities and have been very well received. This provides a reference point for teachers when selecting their texts, along with the flexibility to make their own decisions about what texts to use.

Myth: English teachers will be asked to teach science and social studies reading materials.

Fact: With the ELA standards, English teachers will still teach their students literature as well as literary nonfiction. However, because college and career readiness overwhelmingly focuses on complex texts outside of literature, these standards also ensure students are being prepared to read, write, and research across the curriculum, including in history and science. These goals can be achieved by ensuring that teachers in other disciplines are also focusing on reading and writing to build knowledge within their subject areas.

Myth: The standards do not have enough emphasis on fiction/literature.

Fact: The Common Core requires certain critical content for all students, including classic myths and stories from around the world, America's founding documents, foundational American literature, and Shakespeare. Appropriately, the remaining crucial decisions about what content should be taught are made at the state and local levels. The standards require that a portion of what is read in high school should be informational text, yet the bulk of this portion will be accounted for in non-ELA disciplines that do not frequently use fictional texts. This means that stories, drama, poetry, and other literature account for the majority of reading that students will do in their ELA classes. In addition to content coverage, the standards require that students systematically acquire knowledge in literature and other disciplines through reading, writing, speaking, and listening.

The Myths About Process

Myth: No teachers were involved in writing the standards.

Fact: The Common Core drafting process relied on teachers and standards experts from across the country. In addition, many state experts came together to create the most thoughtful and transparent process of standard setting. This was only made possible by many states working together.

Myth: The standards are not based on research or evidence.

Fact: The standards have made careful use of a large and growing body of evidence. The evidence base includes scholarly research, surveys on what skills are required of students entering college and workforce training programs, assessment data identifying college- and career-ready performance, and comparisons to standards from high-performing states and nations.

In English language arts, the standards build on the firm foundation of the National Assessment of Educational Progress (NAEP) frameworks in reading and writing, which draw on extensive scholarly research and evidence.

In mathematics, the standards draw on conclusions from the Trends in International Mathematics and Science Study (TIMSS) and other studies of high-performing countries that found the traditional U.S. mathematics curriculum needed to become substantially more coherent and focused in order to improve student achievement, addressing the problem of a curriculum that is "a mile wide and an inch deep."

The Myths About Implementation

Myth: The standards tell teachers what to teach.

Fact: Teachers know best about what works in the classroom. That is why these standards establish what students need to learn but do not dictate how teachers should teach. Instead, schools and teachers will decide how best to help students reach the standards.

Myth: Teachers will be left to implement the standards without any support or guidance.

Fact: Decisions on how to implement the standards are made at the state and local levels. As such, states and localities are taking different approaches to implementing the standards and providing their teachers with the supports they need to help students successfully reach the standards. . . .

The Common Core State Standards

The Common Core State Standards for English Language Arts & Literacy in History/Social Studies, Science, and Technical Subjects ("the standards") are the culmination of an extended, broad-based effort to fulfill the charge issued by the states to create the next generation of K–12 standards in order to help ensure that all students are college and career ready in literacy no later than the end of high school.

The present work . . . builds on the foundation laid by states in their decades-long work on crafting high-quality education standards. The standards also draw on the most important international models as well as research and input from numerous sources, including state departments of education, scholars, assessment developers, professional organizations, educators from kindergarten through college, and parents, students, and other members of the public. In their design and content, refined through successive drafts and numerous rounds of feedback, the standards represent a synthesis of the best elements of standards-related work to date and an important advance over that previous work. . . .

The standards are (1) research and evidence based, (2) aligned with college and work expectations, (3) rigorous, and (4) internationally benchmarked. A particular standard was included in the document only when the best available evidence indicated that its mastery was essential for college and career readiness in a twenty-first-century, globally competitive society.

Common Core State Standards Initiative, "Introduction: Common Core State Standards for English Language Arts & Literacy in History/Social Studies, Science, and Technical Subjects," June 2, 2010.

Myth: The standards will be implemented through No Child Left Behind (NCLB) [referring to the No Child Left Behind Act], signifying that the federal government will be leading them.

Fact: The Common Core is a state-led effort that is not part of No Child Left Behind or any other federal initiative. The federal government played no role in the development of the Common Core. State adoption of the standards is in no way mandatory. States began the work to create clear, consistent standards before the American Recovery and Reinvestment Act, which provided funding for the Race to the Top grant program. It also began before the Elementary and Secondary Education Act blueprint was released, because this work is being driven by the needs of the states, not the federal government. . . .

Myth: The Common Core State Standards were adopted by states as part of the Race to the Top grant program.

Fact: Recognizing the strength of having high standards for all students, the federal government gave competitive advantage to Race to the Top applicants that demonstrated that they had or planned to adopt college- and career-ready standards for all students. The program did not specify the Common Core or prevent states from creating their own, separate college- and career-ready standards. States and territories voluntarily chose to adopt the Common Core to prepare their students for college, career, and life. Many states that were not chosen for Race to the Top grants continue to implement the Common Core.

Myth: These standards amount to a national curriculum for our schools.

Fact: The Common Core is *not* a curriculum. It is a clear set of shared goals and expectations for what knowledge and skills will help our students succeed. Local teachers, principals, superintendents, and others will decide how the standards are to be met. Teachers will continue to devise lesson plans and tailor instruction to the individual needs of the students in their classrooms.

Myth: The federal government will take over ownership of the Common Core State Standards Initiative.

Fact: The federal government will *not* govern the Common Core State Standards. The Common Core was and will remain a *state-led* effort. The NGA [National Governors Association] Center [for Best Practices] and CCSSO [Council of Chief State School Officers] are committed to developing a long-term governance structure with leadership from governors, chief state school officers, and other state policy makers to ensure the quality of the Common Core and that teachers and principals have a strong voice in the future of the standards. States and local school districts will drive implementation of the Common Core.

Myth: The Common Core State Standards will result in a national database of private student information.

Fact: There are no data collection requirements for states adopting the standards. Standards define expectations for what students should know and be able to do by the end of each grade. Implementing the Common Core State Standards does not require data collection. The means of assessing students and the use of the data that result from those assessments are up to the discretion of each state and are separate and unique from the Common Core.

VIEWPOINT 2

> *"Pushback against a system now abusing the young and wasting their potential is decades overdue."*

Why Common Core Isn't the Answer

Marion Brady

In the following viewpoint, Marion Brady argues that the Common Core State Standards Initiative should be opposed because the standards are fundamentally in opposition to the aim of schooling. Brady contends that the focus on dividing education into fields of study and then testing those individual fields discourages holistic, systemically integrated thinking that is so crucial to education. He contends that the Common Core standards, among other recent education policy, has stymied educational progress and needs to end. Brady is a newspaper columnist, retired educator, and author of What's Worth Learning?

As you read, consider the following questions:

1. According to Brady, what is the main aim of schooling?
2. What is the reason that nothing can be understood in isolation, according to the author?

Marion Brady, "Why Common Core Isn't the Answer," *Answer Sheet* (blog), *Washington Post*, January 21, 2014. www.washingtonpost.com.

3. Brady believes that what individuals are the only ones with enough clout to exercise political power effectively to change education policy?

As far as I know, no one has asked the general public's opinion about the Common Core State Standards [Initiative] for school subjects. My guess would be that if polled, most people—including most educators—would say they just make good sense.

Opposition to the Standards

But not everyone is a fan. Few oppose standards, but a significant number oppose the Common Core State Standards. Those on the political right don't like the fact that—notwithstanding the word "State" in the title—it was really the feds who helped to railroad the standards into place.

Resisters on the political left cite a range of reasons for opposing the standards—that they were shoved into place without research or pilot programs, that they're a setup for national testing, that the real winners are manufacturers of tests and teaching materials because they can crank out the same stuff for everybody—just to begin a considerably longer list.

Three cheers for those on the political right. Three more for those on the left. May the chaos in Washington and state capitols over education policy help the public realize that, in matters educational, the leaders of business and industry and the politicians who listen to them are blind bulls in china shops.

The Main Aim of Schooling

I began pointing out problems with subject-matter standards beginning with a 1966 article in an education journal, the *Phi Delta Kappan*, and have been at it ever since. A link to a list on my home page summarizes a few of the problems. Here, however, I want to focus on just one problem which, unless it's addressed, could ultimately be fatal to the education system.

I'll start by affirming what I believe most thoughtful educators take for granted: The main aim of schooling is to model or explain reality better. As you read, don't lose sight of that. The aim of schooling isn't to teach math, science, language arts, and other school subjects better, but to expand our understanding of reality.

When I use the word "reality," I'm being concrete and specific. What I can see out of the window directly in front of me is a slice of it. I live on the west bank of the Indian River Lagoon on Florida's east coast. Not really a river, the lagoon is a body of brackish water that stretches fifty or so miles north and about twice that to the south. Off the end of my dock, it's about two miles wide.

This bit of reality cost me money, and continues to do so, but its moods are a source of pleasure, its sunrises are often spectacular, and its easy access by boat to some local restaurants, the Atlantic Ocean and the rest of the world are all pluses. I have, then, reasons to try to understand this particular bit of reality. (Be patient. I'm getting to the point.)

One Particular Bit of Reality

Thirty years ago, when I started building my house, I could often almost walk across the river stepping from clam boat to clam boat. The only clam boats I see now are on trailers in backyards.

Buoys marking underwater crab traps used to dot the river. The traps are gone because most of the crabs are gone.

There was a time when the fish in the lagoon were so plentiful I've had dinner-sized mullet jump into my boat. That no longer happens.

Sea grasses used to cover much of the lagoon's sandy bottom. Now, the stretch of grassless sand that says the lagoon is sick extends for perhaps a quarter of a mile beyond my dock and keeps expanding. All else being equal, my property is losing value.

What's happened? Here's an oversimplified version:

1. When I began building my house, only one house light was visible at night across the river on Merritt Island. Mangrove thickets lined the shore for miles in both directions. Now, there are dozens of lights, and many manicured lawns stretch down to the water's edge.

2. Much of the property on both sides of the river (including mine) isn't part of a municipality. Everyone has a septic system.

3. The soil up and down the coast is mostly sand. The outflow from septic tanks, and the fertilizers and chemicals used to maintain lawns, easily percolate down to the water table, then seep into the river.

4. Nitrogen and phosphorus compounds in the fertilizer and sewage feed unnatural algae blooms, blocking the light from sea grasses and using up dissolved oxygen needed by marine life.

5. Dead organisms turn into black muck, discouraging new grass growth.

6. Property owners, reasoning that their fertilizer and sewage have negligible effect, say, "I'm taxed enough already. Why should I pay for sewage lines and treatment plants?"

The Relationships Between Fields

As I said, I have a serious stake in understanding the reality I've been describing. Unfortunately, no subject in the core curriculum can give me that understanding. I have to assemble it myself using content drawn from demography, geology, botany, mathematics, sociology, law, chemistry, hydraulics, political science, psychology, economics, meteorology, and other fields.

Then comes the hard part—*exploring the relationships between those fields.*

Choose something to think about—anything—and the above applies. Whatever you've chosen to understand can't be thoroughly understood in isolation because it's part of a system. That system will have many parts, the whole will be greater than the sum of those parts, and, to add to the sense-making challenge, the whole is dynamic. While you're trying to make sense of it, it's changing.

Compared to most of the complex realities facing humankind, what's happening to the reality visible out my window is small potatoes. But making sense of it (and *all other realities*) requires a particular kind of thinking—a kind of thinking that makes civilized life possible. *However, the Common Core standards don't promote that kind of thinking. That means it won't get taught, which means it won't get tested, which means we're not really educating, which means too much to even try to summarize.*

The Problem with the Educational System

This is why Alfred North Whitehead, in his 1916 presidential address to the Mathematical Association of England, told educators they needed to "eradicate the fatal disconnection of subjects which kills the vitality of the modern curriculum."

This is why Harlan Cleveland wrote: "It is a well-known scandal that our whole educational system is geared more to categorizing and analyzing patches of knowledge than to threading them together."

This is why John Goodlad, after a massive, multiyear study of American high schools culminating in a 1984 McGraw-Hill book titled *A Place Called School*, wrote, "The division into subjects and periods encourages a segmented rather than an integrated view of knowledge. Consequently, what students are asked to relate to in schooling becomes increasingly artificial, cut off from the human experiences subject matter is supposed to reflect."

This is why dozens of other scholars have been saying the same thing for at least the last several hundred years: What we're doing isn't working!

The systemic nature of reality, the seamless way the brain perceives it, the organizing process that aids memory, the relating process that creates new knowledge, the conceptual networking that yields fresh insights, the meshing of two seemingly unrelated ideas that underlies creativity—all rely on holistic, systemically integrated and related thought. *And it's not being taught.*

The Need to Change Current Policy

Before today's education "reformers"—in a spectacular fit of hubris—took over America's schools, progress in modeling reality more simply and accurately was being made based on general systems theory as it had developed during World War II. No Child Left Behind [Act] and Race to the Top kissed that progress goodbye. Policy makers assume there's nothing wrong with the core curriculum adopted in 1893, so shut up and study, kids.

We can work our way out of the hole we've dug for ourselves, but it can't be done by following orders handed down by authorities in Washington and state capitols, orders that ignore the nature of knowledge, the history of education, the wisdom of hard-earned expertise, the conclusions of research, the nature of human nature, simple management principles, and common sense.

Pushback against a system now abusing the young and wasting their potential is decades overdue. Teachers need autonomy, freedom to experiment, and opportunities for meaningful dialogue with each other and the communities they serve that they don't now have. For most, however, pushing back in today's economy and retribution-prone school culture comes at a price few can afford to pay.

Political power must be exercised, but parents, grandparents, and thoughtful, caring citizens are the only ones with enough clout to exercise it effectively. They need to recognize poor policy when they see it, organize, and act appropriately.

VIEWPOINT 3

> *"Instead of putting taxpayers on the hook for more federal spending, school districts should trim bureaucracy and work on long-term reform options for better targeting taxpayer resources."*

Federal Spending on Education Should Be Limited

Lindsey M. Burke

In the following viewpoint, Lindsey M. Burke argues that no more federal money should be spent on education and that national lawmakers should end federal education programs. Burke contends that state and local governments should take responsibility for education spending and cut bureaucracy by eliminating certain nonteaching staff. She argues that parents and other taxpayers want less money spent on bureaucracy and that it is possible to cut expenses in that realm without sacrificing education quality. Burke is a Will Skillman Fellow in Education at the Heritage Foundation.

As you read, consider the following questions:

1. The percentage of teachers as a portion of school staff has decreased by what since 1950, according to Burke?

Lindsey M. Burke, "How Escalating Education Spending Is Killing Crucial Reform," *Backgrounder*, no. 2739, October 15, 2012.

2. According to Burke, have student-teacher ratios been increasing or declining over the past five decades?

3. According to the author, what percentage of respondents to a recent survey wanted district-level school administrators reduced to the bare minimum?

The [Barack] Obama administration has proposed spending $60 billion on new education programs—in addition to its budget request of nearly $70 billion for fiscal year (FY) 2013 for the U.S. Department of Education. Part of the proposal includes $25 billion specifically to "provide support for hundreds of thousands of education jobs" in order to "keep teachers in the classroom."

Federal Education Spending

In August [2012], the White House released the report "Investing in Our Future: Returning Teachers to the Classroom" to bolster President Barack Obama's call for the $25 billion in new federal spending. The report suggests that, absent a massive new infusion of federal spending, the nation's public schools will face reductions in teaching staff, increases in class size, and a loss of education programs.

However, teaching and nonteaching staff positions in public schools across the country have increased at far greater rates than student enrollment over the past four decades. From 1970 to 2010, student enrollment increased by a modest 7.8 percent, while the number of public school teachers increased by 60 percent. During the same time, nonteaching staff positions increased by 138 percent, and total staffing grew by 84 percent. Teachers now comprise just half of all public education employees.

Instead of putting taxpayers on the hook for more federal spending, school districts should trim bureaucracy and work on long-term reform options for better targeting taxpayer resources.

Education Employees and Student Enrollment

The White House report states that "[a]s teacher jobs are declining, student enrollment is projected to continue growing." A look at the historical data is useful for interpreting the administration's claims.

While enrollment in America's public schools has not quite doubled since 1950, staff positions (both instructional and administrative) increased by 377 percent between 1950 and 2010 (a nearly fivefold increase). From 1970 to 2010, enrollment in the nation's public schools increased just 7.8 percent; over the same time period, education staff increased 84 percent.

More teachers now teach fewer students than at any point in history. The National Center for Education Statistics (housed within the U.S. Department of Education) projects 3.3 million teachers on school payrolls this fall. If accurate, the number of teachers will have increased 261 percent since 1950 and 60 percent since 1970.

While student enrollment is projected to reach 49.6 million this fall—a 5 percent increase since 2000—the number of teachers in the nation's public schools will have grown by 12 percent.

Room to Trim the Budget

The White House report also conflates education jobs with teaching positions, leaving the impression that reductions in staff rolls in the public education system will necessarily lead to fewer teachers in the classroom. While many school districts face potential staff reductions, the growth in nonteaching staff over the past five decades should inform decisions about education staffing and spending.

Over the past five decades, the number of teachers as a percentage of school staff has declined substantially. Since

2000, the percentage of teachers as a portion of school staff has decreased by nearly 3 percent; since 1970, that percentage has declined by 16.5 percent. Notably, the percentage of teachers as a portion of school staff has decreased more than 28 percent since 1950.

This evidence of significant administrative bloat in the nation's public schools should inform staffing decisions. Not surprisingly, increases in the number of administrators have not led to improvements in academic outcomes. Despite significant increases in the proportion of administrative staff to students over the past four to five decades, academic achievement and graduation rates have shown little to no improvement.

Increases in administrative and noninstructional staff over the decades have been substantial. From 1950 to 2009, there was a 68 percent decrease in the ratio of students to school support staff, such as district administration support and library staff. (That figure declined by 42 percent between 1970 and 2009.)

From 1950 to 2009, there was also a 50 percent reduction in the student–principal/assistant principal ratio. (That figure declined by 42 percent from 1970 to 2009.) Over the same time period, there was a 52 percent decrease in the pupil–district administrator ratio. (That figure declined by 49 percent since 1970.)

These decreases indicate that there are more school administrators, support staff, and district employees per student, by a considerable degree, than there were 60 or even 40 years ago. Teachers now comprise just half of all public school employees.

Student-Teacher Ratios in Context

The White House's report cites data from 2008 through 2010 that show a 4.6 percent increase in the student-teacher ratio. The authors of the report warn that local government reductions in the number of education employees will likely lead to further increases in the student-teacher ratio in classrooms across the country:

> A look at the available data shows that the nationwide student-teacher ratio increased by 4.6 percent from the fall of 2008 to the fall of 2010, from 15.3 to 16.0. . . . [T]his increase in the student-teacher ratio erased a decade of gains. Moreover, since the fall of 2010, the last date for which we have the student-teacher ratio data, local governments have cut about 150,000 additional education jobs—meaning that the student-teacher ratio has almost certainly increased further.

Yet, the student-teacher ratio has not "almost certainly increased further" based on preliminary 2012 data from the National Center for Education Statistics (NCES). The NCES finds that "public school systems will employ about 3.3 million full-time-equivalent (FTE) teachers this fall, such that the number of pupils per FTE teacher—that is, the pupil/teacher ratio—will be 15.2. This ratio is lower than the 2000 ratio of 16.0." At 3.3 million, public schools will have a historically high number of teachers in the classrooms this fall. Moreover, the NCES data reveal historically low student-teacher ratios.

In addition to data reported by the NCES, long-term trends in student-teacher ratios provide important context for understanding the current school employment landscape. Assuming the 16:1 figure cited in the White House report (based on 2010 data), the student-teacher ratio has in fact increased by 4.6 percent since 2008, as the report states. But that ratio has *decreased* by 29 percent since 1970 (at which time the student-teacher ratio was a little over 22:1). Since 1950, the student-teacher ratio has declined by more than 40 percent (down from nearly 27:1).

Student-teacher ratios have been on the decline over the past five decades. They are lower than they were in the 1950s and 1970s. The Obama administration's "Investing in Our Future" does state that "since the fall of 2010 . . . local governments have cut about 150,000 additional education jobs—meaning that the student-teacher ratio has almost certainly increased further." But data from fall 2012 projections by the NCES suggest that the student-teacher ratio will actually be at historic lows. Considering data from the NCES estimates, the number of students per teacher will be lower than at any point over the past decade.

Even if student-teacher ratios did increase slightly as the Obama administration projects, it is not clear that further reducing class sizes—or allowing student-teacher ratios to increase modestly—would have any impact on student achievement.

Impact of Class Size on Student Achievement

A Brookings Institution report notes:

> When school finances are limited, the cost-benefit test any educational policy must pass is not "Does this policy have any positive effect?" but rather "Is this policy the most productive use of these educational dollars?" . . . There is no research from the U.S. that directly compares [class size reduction (CSR)] to specific alternative investments, but one careful analysis of several educational interventions found CSR to be the least cost-effective of those studied.

While some evaluations of class size reduction, such as the scientifically rigorous Student-Teacher Achievement Ratio (STAR), have found, under very specific circumstances, positive benefits on student achievement from smaller class sizes, research by economist Eric Hanushek found a limited impact on academic achievement, with gains fading out by sixth grade and beyond. Researchers Matthew Chingos and Caroline Hoxby found no impact on student achievement resulting from reductions in class size. The NCES also found that "overall the evidence of the effects of differences in class size on student performance is weak."

The NCES further reports that the United States has the lowest elementary student–teacher ratio of any G8 country except Italy. South Korea, which consistently outperforms the United States on international assessments, has an average student-teacher ratio of 30:1.

Continuing to lower student-teacher ratios places a tremendous financial burden on state taxpayers for little, if any, academic benefit. As the Brookings Institution further explains:

> [I]ncreasing the pupil/teacher ratio in the U.S. by one student would save at least $12 billion per year in teacher salary costs alone, which is roughly equivalent to the outlays of Title I of the Elementary and Secondary Education Act, the federal government's largest single K–12 education program.

Student-Teacher Ratios vs. Class Size

It is important to note the difference between student-teacher ratio and class size. Student-teacher ratio refers to the number of students per full-time teacher in a given school. The NCES measures student-teacher ratios "by dividing the number of full-time-equivalent students at a given level of education by the number of full-time-equivalent teachers at that level." These measurements exclude paraprofessionals, such as teachers' aides.

By contrast, class size refers to the number of students in a class (an algebra or English class, for example), and can include both the teacher and a teacher's aide in the room. The NCES defines average class size as "the division of students who are following a common course of study, based on the highest number of common courses."

While student-teacher ratios are usually lower than average class size, the NCES has tracked student-teacher ratios over time, making the measure a valuable tool for evaluation.

Reductions in education jobs, if that is the case, do not mean that the student-teacher ratio "has almost certainly increased further," as the White House claims. Even if such reductions were to take place, leading to nominal increases in the student-teacher ratio, such an increase is unlikely to have an adverse effect on student achievement.

Moreover, the administration's rhetoric concerning student-teacher ratios and class size implies that cuts in education jobs affect teachers exclusively. States, however, have ample room to reduce—and in fact should reduce—nonteaching staff positions, which have grown significantly over the past four decades.

A Better Plan for Relieving School Budgets

Funding education is a state and local government responsibility. Continuing to increase federal funding ensures that Washington intervention into education will continue to grow, at the expense of parents, taxpayers, and local school leaders. Rather than spending $25 billion in taxpayer money through yet another federal education program, the federal government should empower states with more flexibility and control over how existing federal education dollars are spent. National policy makers should:

- *Allow states to opt out of federal K–12 programs authorized under the Elementary and Secondary Education Act and to direct funding to the education programs of their choice.* The Academic Partnerships Lead Us to Success (A-PLUS) Act, introduced in Congress in both 2007 and 2011, has these goals. It allows states to opt out of No Child Left Behind [Act] and use funding for any lawful education purpose that a state sees as most necessary. Not only does this approach give states greater

Growth in Education Staffing and Student Enrollment

Since 1970, total student enrollment in public schools increased by 3.7 million, or 8 percent. However, during that same period, total education staffing rose by 2.8 million, or 84 percent. Most notable was the growth in non-teaching staff, which increased by 138 percent.

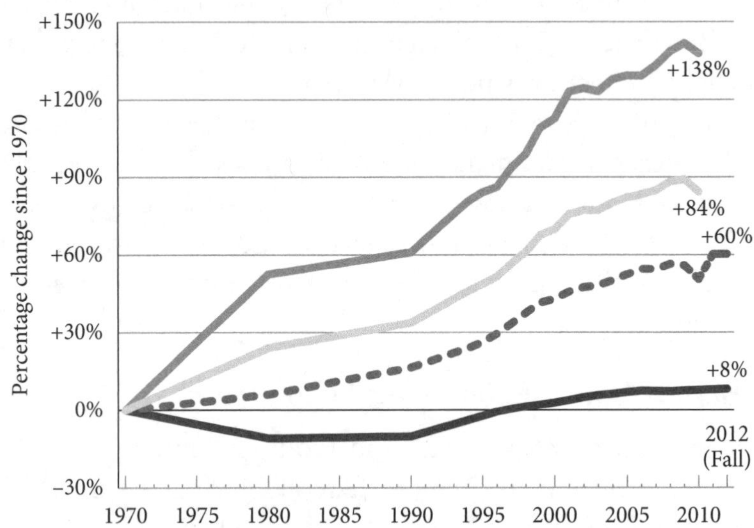

Notes: Some figures have been interpolated. Figures for teachers and student enrollment for 2011 and fall 2012 are projected.

Original sources: National Center for Education Statistics, Digest of Education Statistics, "Staff employed in public elementary and secondary school systems, by functional area: Selected years, 1949-50 through fall 2009," Table 85, http://nces.ed.gov/programs/digest/d11/tables/dt11_085.asp (accessed August 30, 2012); Digest of Education Statistics 2011, June 2012, http://nces.ed.gov/pubs2012/2012001.pdf (accessed August 30, 2012); and National Center for Education Statistics, "The Condition of Education 2012," May 2012, http://nces.ed.gov/pubs2012/2012045.pdf (accessed August 30, 2012).

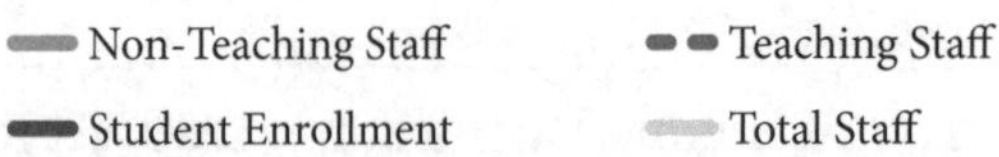

TAKEN FROM: Lindsey M. Burke, "How Escalating Education Spending Is Killing Crucial Reform," Heritage Foundation, *Backgrounder*, no. 2739, October 15, 2012.

flexibility and control over their education dollars, it also eliminates many of the costs associated with administering federal programs and complying with the accompanying requirements.

- *Simplify federal education programs and increase funding flexibility.* The U.S. Department of Education should simplify Title I and other formula grants. While Title I provides funding to low-income school districts, its complex and multiple-funding streams make it more difficult for dollars to reach students. Consolidating the funding streams and simplifying the application and reporting requirements of Title I would save states time and money that could be better directed toward the classroom. States should also be allowed to make federal Title I dollars portable if they choose, following a child to any school of choice.

There are also numerous state-level reforms that should be pursued, which would likely reduce budget shortfalls while improving the education landscape. State policy makers should:

- *Reduce the number of noninstructional and administrative positions in public schools.* States should consider cutting costs in areas that are long overdue for reform and pursue systemic reform to improve student achievement. Specifically, states should refrain from continuing to increase the number of nonteaching staff in public schools.

- *Eliminate "last-in, first-out" policies.* Too many states continue to use seniority-based layoffs when making staffing decisions. These last-in, first-out (LIFO) policies should be abandoned in favor of staffing decisions based on teacher effectiveness and competence, not years spent in the school building.

- *Avoid across-the-board pay raises.* The average public school teacher receives total compensation above his similarly skilled private-sector counterpart. For that reason, state and local policy makers should avoid across-the-board pay raises and should instead revamp teacher compensation systems to better reward those teachers who have a positive impact on student performance.
- *Allow alternative teacher certification and reciprocity of teacher licensure.* Barriers to entry into the teaching profession, such as certification, should be eliminated. If a state continues to require certification, credentialing through alternative teacher certification organizations, such as the American Board for Certification of Teacher Excellence, should be honored as a means for entering the teaching profession. Licensure should also be reciprocal; licensure in any state should be valid in any other state. While the barrier to entering the profession should be lowered, states and local schools should make their own teacher evaluations much more rigorous upon classroom entry.

What Taxpayers Want

A recent survey conducted by the [Thomas B.] Fordham Institute found that 69 percent of respondents supported "reducing the number of district level administrators to the bare minimum" if their school district was facing a budget shortfall. Parents and taxpayers have good reason to want to trim bureaucracy in their local public schools. From 1970 to 2010, student enrollment increased by a modest 7.8 percent, while the number of public school teachers increased by 60 percent. During that same time period, nonteaching staff positions increased by 138 percent, and total staffing grew by 84 percent.

Not surprisingly, the more than doubling of nonteaching staff since 1970 has meant that teachers are a smaller proportion of school payrolls. Since 1970, the percentage of teachers as a portion of school staff has declined by 16.5 percent. Teachers now comprise just half of all public school employees.

More teachers are teaching fewer students, as the student-teacher ratio has continued to decline. According to the NCES, the student-teacher ratio for fall 2012 will be slightly greater than 15:1.

The Obama administration's call for $25 billion in new federal funding for education salaries is based on a small snapshot of data (for 2008–2010) that shows overall reductions in education staff, which it then conflates with teaching positions specifically.

Another federal education bailout will act as a disincentive for state and local education leaders to make the changes necessary for long-term reform and balanced budgets, and further obliges taxpayers to fund policies of dubious value.

VIEWPOINT 4

> *"State governments can create more opportunities by ensuring adequate levels of spending, an appropriate proportion of funding from the state, and greater spending equity."*

Government Spending on Education Needs to Be More Equitable

Marin Gjaja, J. Puckett, and Matt Ryder

In the following viewpoint, Marin Gjaja, J. Puckett, and Matt Ryder argue that new research shows that there is a correlation between education spending and outcomes. The authors contend that increased spending has positive results on education outcomes, a greater proportion of spending by the state on education improves outcomes, and increased funding equity positively impacts low-income students' performance. Gjaja is a senior partner and managing director in the Boston Consulting Group's Chicago office; J. Puckett is a senior partner and managing director in the firm's Dallas office; and Matt Ryder is a consultant in the Chicago office.

Marin Gjaja, J. Puckett, and Matt Ryder, "When It Comes to School Funding, Equity Is the Key," *Education Week*, vol. 33, February 19, 2014, pp. 30–31.

As you read, consider the following questions:

1. The authors studied the impact of education spending on the outcomes of what assessment?
2. Increasing the proportion of education funding covered by the state resulted in the most pronounced gains in what subject for what students, according to the authors?
3. The authors contend that making their three proposed changes to education funding would result in higher tests scores for low-income students by what amount?

The relationship between government spending on K–12 public education and student outcomes has been an endless source of debate among those involved in education policy.

The Correlation Between Spending and Outcomes

For example, the United States spends more on education than any other industrialized country, yet ranks at or below average in the latest international math, science, and reading scores, compared with the world's most developed countries.

Some argue that there is no correlation between spending and outcomes. But new research from our management consulting firm, the Boston Consulting Group [BCG], adds another dimension to the discussion. BCG has worked in numerous school systems and states and has analyzed issues of school funding, student performance, and equity for years.

In our ongoing work with Advance Illinois (a nonprofit education advocacy organization whose board includes one of us, Marin Gjaja), recently we looked at state funding of public education. Our analysis led us to investigate the relationship between the way each of the 50 states funds K–12 public education and that state's student outcomes on the National Assessment of Educational Progress [NAEP]. We focused on 4th grade reading scores and 8th grade math scores from 2003 to 2011, and we also looked at outcomes for students at different income levels. We controlled for regional variations in costs between states as well as for the differences in the concentrations of poverty.

The Impact of Spending

We found that how much state governments spend per pupil and how they spend it does in fact have a significant correlation with achievement, particularly for the low-income students whose performance on average significantly lags behind that of students from more advantaged backgrounds. We also discovered strong statistical evidence to support three findings about the relationship between state-level funding and student outcomes. Each of these insights can inform the debates about K–12 public education spending at the local, state, and federal levels.

The level of spending matters. Our analysis shows that increased spending per pupil has a positive impact on 4th grade reading results, both for low-income students and their non-low-income peers. Our statistical modeling predicted that, all else remaining equal, a $1,000-per-pupil funding increase is correlated with a .42-point increase in NAEP scores for low-income 4th graders.

In the current challenged fiscal environment, states and districts are sometimes reducing spending on education, hoping that a little belt-tightening will not affect student performance. Our research predicts that the dollars being reallocated to address other spending priorities at the state or local level are likely to have a negative impact on all schoolchildren and will hurt low-income students the most.

The Importance of State Spending

The source of spending matters. The proportion of public education spending provided by state governments varies widely across the United States. Significant funding also comes from the federal government, local property taxes, and additional fund-raising among parents and the community, particularly in wealthier districts. We found that the greater the proportion of total public spending covered by a state, the better the outcomes on NAEP.

The effect was most pronounced for the 8th grade math scores of low-income students. Our model showed, at 99 percent confidence, that an increase of 20 percentage points in the state share of spending correlated with a 1-point improvement in the 8th grade math scores of low-income students.

In most states, local property taxes tend to stay in the local district and cannot be redirected outside that district toward those in greatest need as easily as state funding can.

States can help level the playing field by directing spending across a much wider and more diverse area than a local district. Those states paying a low share of total education spending are not using the power of the purse to most efficiently allocate funding to the highest needs.

The Importance of Equity

The equity of spending matters. By far, the most statistically robust finding in our analysis was the role of increased funding equity in student outcomes.

Equity should require that every student receives sufficient resources to have the same chance to succeed, rather than that every child gets the same level of funding. Unfortunately, many states are far from achieving even the same level of funding for students at different incomes. Many states are in fact quite inequitable in how they allocate education funding, paradoxically investing much more in the richest students than they do in the poorest students, as a result of a combination of complex state spending formulas and a heavy reliance on local funding.

Giving kids in high-poverty areas an equal opportunity to succeed requires spending more money on those students. We have observed that states with increased equity ratios (the ratio of per-student funding between high- and low-poverty districts) have had a positive impact on low-income students' performance in reading and math. In fact, we have found that increased funding equity benefits students at every income level.

Many districts have a wide range of student income backgrounds, so greater funding for low-income districts benefits both low- and high-income students.

Interestingly, our analysis suggests that an improvement in the equity of funding across a state can improve academic performance without any additional spending overall. And the effect is significant: For example, a 20-point improvement in the equity ratio, holding all other factors constant, is correlated with nearly 2-point improvement in 4th grade NAEP reading scores for low-income students, equal to a roughly 1 percent gain.

The Questions for Policy Makers

By optimizing all three of these elements, our modeling predicts that states can increase NAEP scores for low-income students by 1 percent to 2 percent. That may not sound like a lot, but in some states such a gain would bring as many as a quarter of low-income kids who were formerly not proficient in reading to proficiency. Given the connection between proficiency and college readiness, the odds of low-income students completing college would consequently be higher. Hundreds of thousands of kids would have a better chance at academic and career success.

But to get the funding formula right for public education, policy makers need to ask themselves the following set of broad questions:

- Are all kids and all districts getting adequate funding in the aggregate?

- Is the state's proportion of spending great enough to help level the playing field?
- Is state funding equitable (not equal) across districts?

The United States can better live up to its reputation as the land of opportunity by creating more opportunities for all students, especially low-income students. State governments can create more opportunities by ensuring adequate levels of spending, an appropriate proportion of funding from the state, and greater spending equity. Changes in these areas can maximize the impact of resources spent on education, fostering better student outcomes and changing lives.

VIEWPOINT 5

> *"The first line of attack should always be to knock out inefficient monopolies that hamper the efficiency of all school districts."*

Teachers' Unions Should Be Eliminated

Richard A. Epstein

In the following viewpoint, Richard A. Epstein argues that a recent court decision in California was right to diminish the power of teachers' unions; however, he claims, the decision did not go far enough. He contends that the public trust doctrine requires that states stop engaging in collective bargaining with all entities, especially educators. Epstein is the Laurence A. Tisch Professor of Law at New York University School of Law and the Peter and Kirsten Bedford Senior Fellow at the Hoover Institution.

As you read, consider the following questions:

1. According to the author, what three practices in the standard teachers' union contract did the California judge strike down?

Richard A. Epstein, "A Win for Students," *Defining Ideas*, June 17, 2014.

2. The entire system of collective bargaining negotiations leads to what result, according to Epstein?
3. What is the "public trust doctrine," according to the author?

The recent decision [June 10, 2014] of Judge Rolf M. Treu in *Vergara v. [State of California]* has sent shudders through California's once invincible unions. The plaintiff's statewide student class-action lawsuit was led by accomplished lawyer Theodore Boutrous on behalf of the reformist group Students Matter, whose activities have been heavily funded by Silicon Valley mogul David F. Welch.

Judge Treu's decision struck down three essential pillars of the standard teachers' union contract. It first took aim at the standard California teachers' contract, which awards tenure after as little as 16 months of services. It next gave a thumbs-down to the elaborate procedural devices a school district has to go through to dismiss a teacher for incompetence. As Student Matters reports: "Out of 275,000 teachers statewide, 2.2 teachers are dismissed for unsatisfactory performance per year on average, which amounts to 0.0008 percent." Finally, *Vergara* nixed the current "last in, first out" seniority system, under which the only grounds for dismissing a teacher is the reverse order in which they are hired, wholly without regard to classroom performance and subject matter need. All of these practices undercut the effectiveness of student education and waste taxpayer dollars. This is why educational professionals like Secretary of Education Arne Duncan are supporting the California decision, to the immense dissatisfaction of Randi Weingarten, president of the American Federation of Teachers.

The Role of Teacher Unions

The California teachers' union justifies these rules on the ground that they are needed to combat the danger that craven public school administrators will resort to arbitrary and vindictive personnel decisions on such vital topics as hiring, firing, assignments, pay, promotion, and punishment. The rigid union contract serves as a protection against such so-called arbitrariness. It is notable, of course, that all nonunion businesses, in education and elsewhere, confer far greater levels of discretion to management without personnel being abused left and right.

The two key elements that unions leave out of their equation are reputation and competition. A school district, or indeed any employer, who acts as irrationally as the teachers' union assumes that principals and administrators will not be able to recruit or retain the teachers whom it wants. Bad news travels fast, and competitive forces will go a long way to restrain abuse by offering contracts that develop more sensible grievance procedures to deal with matters of employee discipline and dismissal. Indeed, one serious downside of unionized schools is that they have to hire administrators who can endure the rigors of collective bargaining negotiations and constant scrapes with aggressive union representatives. The cycle thus feeds on itself, as disgruntled teachers can point to unwise administrative decisions that make teachers boiling mad and stoke yet another pro-union burst of support.

In this difficult setting, education takes a back seat to potential strikes and archaic work rules. None of these persistent problems arise in nonunion charter schools, where management issues are handled with a great deal more aplomb than in the union context. The proof here is in the pudding. Union schools are stagnant operations in which bad schools never fail. But the charter school market is far more dynamic. As Karl Zinsmeister reported some months ago in the *Wall Street Journal*, both failure and success receive their just desserts in the charter school market, which explains why their performance has dramatically improved in recent years: "Nationwide, 561 new charter schools opened last year, while 206 laggards were closed."

The large charter school networks develop replicable models whose test scores now clearly outperform those of public schools with entrenched financial support. There is a waiting list for getting in to charter schools; there is clearly a demand for their services. Sound public policy would encourage their maximum development, which would reduce the high taxes paid to trap children of all backgrounds in inferior public schools. With the help of charters, competition will dominate the state-created monopolies in education.

A Constitutional Question

In many ways, the most difficult challenge in this case is to come up with a credible constitutional theory that explains why Judge Treu should have intervened as he did. The provisions of the California constitution are not obviously adapted to this particular task. It contains the standard federal constitutional guarantees of due process and equal protection, and two other provisions that deal with the operation of the educational system in more general terms.

> SECTION 1. A general diffusion of knowledge and intelligence being essential to the preservation of the rights and liberties of the people, the Legislature shall encourage by all suitable means the promotion of intellectual, scientific, moral, and agricultural improvement.

> SECTION 5. The Legislature shall provide for a system of common schools by which a free school shall be kept up and supported in each district at least six months in every year, after the first year in which a school has been established.

In *Vergara*, Judge Treu went somewhat over the top in claiming that the shortfalls he found in the current union contracts were reminiscent of the system of segregated schools that the Supreme Court struck down in *Brown v. Board of Education* in 1954. Racial discrimination by the government rightly receives the strictest level of scrutiny on any and all theories of government because it provides an easy axis for unscrupulous politicians to transfer privileges, opportunities, and wealth to their own groups.

No one can claim that union preferences rise to the level of racial discrimination, but their long-term effects are nonetheless insidious, so much so that one can ask the question of how the legislature can encourage the promotion of intellectual and scientific institutions when it voluntarily cedes enormous monopoly power to teachers' unions so that they can bargain for a set of favors that would never be tolerated in a competitive market. And make no mistake about it, that privileged position is exactly what all unions have obtained, not only with respect to the particular terms that were attacked by Judge Treu, but more particularly with respect to the unsustainable pensions that have taken cities like San Jose, with whom I have worked, to the brink of financial ruin. In this regard, the root of the problem is not the particular manifestations of union power struck down in *Vergara*, deplorable as they may be. Rather, it is the entire system of collective bargaining negotiations that leads to the result in which whole student populations, as well as the public, suffer from a system that is designed to entrench special benefits for one group at the expense of the population at large.

The Public Trust Doctrine

The question is how to find some way to attack the underlying disease instead of looking solely at the symptoms, which are all too painful. The serious gap in our constitutional design lies in the simple fact that the document itself contains fairly sensible limitations on the direct application of the traditional government powers of taxation and regulation. But by the same token, the constitutional text is far weaker in imposing limitations on the way in which the government chooses to distribute its benefits in standard market transac-

Statement from US Secretary of Education Arne Duncan Regarding the Decision in *Vergara*

For students in California and every other state, equal opportunities for learning must include the equal opportunity to be taught by a great teacher. The students who brought this lawsuit [*Vergara v. State of California*] are, unfortunately, just nine out of millions of young people in America who are disadvantaged by laws, practices and systems that fail to identify and support our best teachers and match them with our neediest students. Today's court decision is a mandate to fix these problems. Together, we must work to increase public confidence in public education. This decision presents an opportunity for a progressive state with a tradition of innovation to build a new framework for the teaching profession that protects students' rights to equal educational opportunities while providing teachers the support, respect and rewarding careers they deserve. My hope is that today's decision moves from the courtroom toward a collaborative process in California that is fair, thoughtful, practical and swift. Every state, every school district needs to have that kind of conversation. At the federal level, we are committed to encouraging and supporting that dialogue in partnership with states. At the same time, we all need to continue to address other inequities in education—including school funding, access to quality early childhood programs and school discipline.

US Department of Education,
"Statement from U.S. Secretary of Education Arne Duncan Regarding the Decision in Vergara v. California,"
June 10, 2014.

tions. A moment's reflection, however, will show that the risk of government giveaways to favored groups of any description is every bit as substantial as the risk of government expropriation. By way of simple comparison, no corporate board is allowed to enter into sweetheart deals with key officers and directors under which they receive valuable assets for a tiny fraction of their market price. A wide range of derivative actions is made available to shareholders suing in the name of the corporation to unravel the transaction.

Exactly that difficulty arises when legislatures put in place institutions that empower unions to gain monopoly benefits, whether in cash, pensions, or work rules, that come at the expense of both school students and the public at large. In 1987 I wrote an article, "The Public Trust Doctrine," which stood for the proposition "nor shall public property be given away for private use, without just compensation." The public trust doctrine announced by the United States Supreme Court in the 1892 decision of *Illinois Central Railroad v. Illinois* represents an effort to reach that conclusion in connection with land grants, and there is no reason why it cannot apply with equal force to one-sided labor contracts that result when the legislature arms unions with the right to negotiate collective bargaining agreements on behalf of its members. That statutory grant of power against the state for a select group of individuals against the whole represents, in the most literal sense of the term, a per se breach of the duty of loyalty that legislatures owe to their citizens, much as corporate boards owe to their shareholders.

The question then arises of whether this decisive attack on union dominance amounts to a form of unprincipled judicial activism. Just that charge could be leveled against a group of the decisions on which Judge Treu placed great weight: the *Serrano v. Priest* litigation (1971–1977). Those cases required, in the name of equal protection, that the state equalize the finances across all school districts in order to equalize educational opportunities for students. I have serious misgivings about the decision in the *Serrano* line of cases because it rests on a much more dubious theory of government intervention, namely the equal protection clause of the federal Constitution, and the various California provisions, which are intended to secure massive redistribution through judicial power. In this instance, it led to a surrender of local control over school districts that transferred power from parents to the state legislature.

The point here is simple enough. Tread very carefully in dealing with government interventions that want to take wealth from some and give it to others. The first line of attack should always be to knock out inefficient monopolies that hamper the efficiency of all school districts, which has far more unambiguous consequences for social welfare. The difficulty with Judge Treu, then, is that he did not go far enough. Don't just stop with the most invidious provisions of union contracts, but instead knock out the entire system of state collective bargaining and branch.

VIEWPOINT

> *"Teachers' unions are one of the few institutional forces with the power to fight back against austerity and privatization."*

Teachers' Unions Are a Positive Force for Education

Amy B. Dean

In the following viewpoint, Amy B. Dean argues that teachers' unions across the country are involved in educating children holistically. She claims that this illustrates the power of such unions to get teachers involved in the community outside the classroom in order to influence education inside the classroom in a positive manner. Dean is a fellow of the Century Foundation and principal of ABD Ventures, which works to develop new strategies for social change organizations. She is the coauthor of A New New Deal: How Regional Activism Will Reshape the American Labor Movement.

As you read, consider the following questions:

1. According to the author, what action do education reformers want to take regarding teachers?

Amy B. Dean, "Protecting Classrooms from Corporate Takeover: What Families Can Learn from Teachers' Unions," *Yes!*, Spring 2014.

2. According to Dean, schools in high-poverty areas produce the most positive outcomes when they occupy what role?
3. What program did the Saint Paul Federation of Teachers start in 2010, according to the author?

Teachers have always held a cherished role in our society—recognized as professionals who know how to inculcate a love of learning in our children. But the "education reform" movement represented by No Child Left Behind [Act] and Race to the Top blames teachers for the problems in our public schools.

"The people who seek to privatize the public sector are looking for any excuse to criticize teachers," says Bob Peterson, veteran fifth-grade teacher and president of the Milwaukee Teachers' Education Association (MTEA). "We must take responsibility for our profession. If we don't step up to the plate, public education is going to be destroyed."

A Debate About the Role of Teachers

At heart, this is a debate between competing visions of teachers' roles in public education in America. Teachers, through their unions, are defending the idea that they are best equipped to teach children to become lifelong learners. Education "reformers," though, cite studies—such as one from the Goldwater Institute from 2004—that show that students at privately run charter schools outperform kids in public schools and say that public education would improve if public schools simply looked more like privately run schools. In privately run schools, teachers lack a collective voice, their working conditions are subject to the whims of school administrators, and they can be fired at will. This contrast with the empowered rank and file of unionized public school teachers could help explain the claims of "reformers" that traditional public school teachers are too sheltered, that they can't be dismissed easily enough, and that their unions need to be eliminated. Firing and replacing teachers based on students' scores on standardized tests, then, is part of the reformers' vision for the schools.

Everyone agrees that great teachers are key to a good education. But reform advocates such as former Washington, D.C., schools chief Michelle Rhee say that schools can fire their way to excellence. In September 2013, according to a report on the public policy website Next City, Rhee spoke at Temple University. Exemplifying the rhetoric of the reformers, Rhee said, "Not everyone can do this job. If you have a pulse and pass the criminal check, a lot of school districts will just stick you in the classroom." But Rhee's approach is to evaluate teachers by giving their students standardized tests. This approach offers, at best, an imprecise evaluation, failing to measure the intangibles that make great teachers. The result is that some of the best teachers get taken out, along with a few bad ones.

Peterson and other educators say that, unsurprisingly, the reformers' approach undermines those who have devoted their professional lives to educating kids. In 2010, Rhee fired 241 D.C. public school teachers in a single day, but failed to achieve the promised turnaround in standardized test scores. The achievement gap between black and white elementary students is now wider than ever, as education writer Dana Goldstein and others have noted since Rhee's departure from D.C.

Across the country, teachers' unions are fighting back against the work of people like Rhee by working to educate children holistically. This means taking into account all the factors that influence students' chances for success: families, homes, communities, and often the effects of poverty. In Milwaukee, Peterson is working with his union to emphasize teacher professionalism and social justice in the community. In New York City, as part of a union-based program, 16 schools have reinvented themselves as hubs for community services. In St. Paul, teachers visit parents in their homes to build engagement with families.

A Union's Efforts in Milwaukee Schools

Peterson's organizing efforts in Milwaukee focus on highlighting how the interests of teachers—for instance, having paid time for class preparation—align closely with those of students. Peterson is a longtime fifth-grade teacher and former editor of the progressive education magazine *Rethinking Schools*. He was elected president of the MTEA representing a caucus of teachers who advocate funding and fixing public schools. His organizing efforts focus on using the union's clout not merely to protect teachers' jobs but to champion the common interests of teachers, students, parents, and the community.

As a first change, the union actively encourages teachers to work for social justice in their communities. "In the past, our union didn't really do much outreach to the community except when we needed support for our issues," Peterson says. "That's changed." Recently, Peterson says, MTEA teachers turned out to support immigrants' rights groups in the city alongside a grassroots organization called Voces de la Frontera and provided adult advising and mentoring for its youth arm, Youth Empowered in the Struggle. Union members also joined picket lines in spring 2012 in support of striking Palermo's pizza factory workers. These are not actions that seem directly related to education. For MTEA teachers, addressing such stressors as legal status, support in the community, and economic insecurity is critical to student success. "We are really trying to change the narrative in the community," he says, "from 'teacher unions just defend bad teachers' to a narrative where we are seen as the go-to people when it comes to public education."

In the schools, the union's focus is on making clear how, in Peterson's words, "our teaching conditions are our students' learning conditions." The union's negotiating team recently won a 50 percent increase in paid class preparation time for MTEA teachers, allowing the teachers to accommodate the more complex curriculum material that will boost their students' achievement.

A final leg of the union's efforts, Peterson argues, is to "reclaim our profession in our classrooms." Teachers "should be child-driven and data-informed," Peterson says, using a broad set of data to measure the success of the whole child, rather than measuring learning strictly with standardized tests. In one example, the union lent its voice to the effort to overhaul Milwaukee's ailing early childhood education system and convened a joint task force with school officials to lay the groundwork for improvements in the city's pre-K through third-grade programs. Recognizing the strong evidence that improved early childhood teaching makes for improved long-term outcomes for all kids, the union has assigned early childhood education experts to the task force.

The Community School Model

Because a child's education doesn't start or stop at the classroom door, education and public health officials are moving toward a consensus that schools in high-poverty areas produce the most positive outcomes when they are seamless parts of the community. Members of New York City's United Federation of Teachers (UFT) regularly confront the way poverty interferes with their students' ability to learn. They argue that the right of all children to an education is intertwined with the right of families to live free from hunger and preventable medical problems, and to have access to adequate child care as well as parenting support.

Working with parent leaders, politicians, and school administrators, the UFT is transforming traditional public schools into community schools. The community school model was piloted in New York by the Children's Aid Society and by the Harlem Children's Zone, a comprehensive education program anchored in a partnership with Promise Academy charter schools. The model makes the school a hub where families can be introduced to available services, from child care to medical attention to classes for parents and activities for non-school-age children. In 2012, the UFT announced an initiative, which received $700,000 in new funding from the state, to establish before- and after-school care, medical services, parents' activities, clubs, and sports at 16 existing schools throughout the city.

Similar efforts exist outside New York. Activists from the national American Federation of Teachers (AFT) consulted on a project to open a community school in 2013 in Lawrence, Mass. There, the local AFT affiliate is taking full control of one school, right down to selecting its principal. The school will provide health services and child care, in keeping with the union's vision of broadening the school's role in the community.

Engaging Parents in the Home

The Saint Paul Federation of Teachers is experimenting with reestablishing teachers as partners in a child's learning and development, rather than an external authority. Their parent-teacher home visit project in St. Paul, Minn., started in 2010, is led by science teacher Nick Faber. "The project stands a lot of our traditional parent engagement on its head," Faber says. "We [used to] invite parents in and talk at them, tell them things that we think they don't know. And we'd stand around and wonder why they don't show up." The new program builds relationships, using the first visit for parents and teachers simply to get to know each other and the second visit to build capacity for parents to take on more school leadership, such as joining a committee or helping in the classroom.

Inspired by a similar program in Sacramento, Calif., the St. Paul program started with eight teachers making home visits in 2010. Sixty-six teachers attended the program's trainings in 2011, and Faber reports that more than 300 teachers are now trained to visit students' families. More than 200 visits were completed in just the first two months of the 2013–2014 school year. The national AFT helped Faber start the home visits project with initial funding for training and is now helping him put structural supports—like partnerships with community-based organizations and program evaluations—into place so it can continue to grow.

Teachers' unions are one of the few institutional forces with the power to fight back against austerity and privatization, and to instead insist that our understanding of education must extend well beyond the walls of the classroom. Scapegoating teachers will not get us to an educational model that takes the challenges of the system as a whole into account. Following the example of innovative, teacher-led programs in Milwaukee, New York City, and St. Paul will.

Periodical and Internet Sources Bibliography

The following articles have been selected to supplement the diverse views presented in this chapter.

Jason Bedrick	"Education Excellence Can't Be Achieved from Above," *redefinED*, June 9, 2014.
Andrew J. Coulson	"A Less Perfect Union," *American Spectator*, June 2011.
Eric A. Hanushek	"More Easily Firing Bad Teachers Helps Everyone," *Education Next*, June 12, 2014.
Frederick M. Hess and Andrew P. Kelly	"A Federal Education Agenda," *National Affairs*, no. 13, Fall 2012.
Richard D. Kahlenberg	"Bipartisan, but Unfounded: The Assault on Teachers' Unions," *American Educator*, vol. 35, no. 4, Winter 2011–2012.
Joel Klein	"The Failure of American Schools," *Atlantic*, June 2011.
Terry M. Moe	"The Staggering Power of the Teachers' Unions," *Hoover Digest*, no. 3, July 2011.
Pedro Noguera	"Schools Need More than the Common Core," *Nation*, September 30, 2013.
Amanda Ripley	"Training Teachers to Embrace Reform," *Wall Street Journal*, September 14, 2012.
Reihan Salam	"Why More Federal Education Spending Is Not the Answer," *National Review Online*, April 4, 2014.

Chapter 2

How Should Students, Teachers, and Schools Be Evaluated?

Chapter Preface

During the presidency of George W. Bush, Congress passed the No Child Left Behind Act (NCLB). NCLB requires all public schools that receive federal funding to administer yearly standardized tests of student performance to show that their students are making adequate progress. Each state is able to design its own assessment system and set its own system for measuring yearly progress. NCLB requires states to test students in English, mathematics, and science. States must publicly report test results for all students who took the test, as well as for specific student subgroups, including low-income students, students with disabilities, English language learners, and major racial and ethnic groups.

NCLB also requires states to ensure that all of their public school teachers are "highly qualified." NCLB requires states to issue state teacher licensure exams to get a license to teach in the state. In addition, states must develop assessments for teachers to demonstrate subject-matter competency, ensuring that highly qualified teachers are equally distributed across students of all minorities and income levels.

Although the ability for states to control student and teacher assessment is popular among those who want local control of education policy, critics charge that without national standards there is no reliable way to assess how students are doing from state to state. Allowing each state to develop its own system of standards raises the possibility that one state's standards are drastically lower than another state's standards.

A 2012 Gallup poll found that most Americans do not believe that NCLB has improved education: 16 percent of Americans said that it had made education better, 38 percent believed it had not made much difference, and 29 percent thought that it had made public school education worse. In a

2013 poll by Phi Delta Kappa International (PDK) and Gallup, only 22 percent of Americans said that they believed the significant increase in testing in the public schools to measure academic achievement over the past decade has helped performance, whereas 36 percent said it has hurt student performance.

The majority of Americans polled by PDK/Gallup in October 2014 opposed the practice by states of using student performance on standardized tests in the evaluation of teachers, with 61 percent opposing this practice and 38 percent supporting it. As with the general public, the authors in the following chapter illustrate that opinion is varied on the best way to assess students, teachers, and schools.

VIEWPOINT 1

> *"Our kids and our schools shouldn't have their whole futures riding on how well children can fill in little circles, to be scored by machines."*

Standardized Testing Is Harming Student Learning

Mary Elizabeth Williams

In the following viewpoint, Mary Elizabeth Williams argues that standardized testing has taken over public education. She contends that the current testing requirements are resulting in frightening culture change at schools, where a vast amount of energy is spent getting teachers and students ready for testing. Williams claims that such testing has taken away teachers' ability to teach effectively and has resulted in poorer education for children. She concludes that the strategy of improving education through standardized testing has failed. Williams is a staff writer for Salon.

As you read, consider the following questions:

1. Williams cites a schoolteacher friend who told her that up to what fraction of her salary will be tied to student test results?

Mary Elizabeth Williams, "Testing Is Killing Learning," Salon, April 18, 2013.

2. The author suggests that school administrators may be tempted to engage in intimidation or cheating to get good test outcomes for what reason?
3. Who does Williams contend are the only clear-cut winners in the high-stakes student assessment culture?

It's called a "prep rally." This week [in April 2013], New York public school students are taking their standardized tests, in line with the national Common Core learning standards. Last week, the principal of my third grader's progressive, learn-by-doing school sent home a letter about the "overemphasis on assessments and the unintended consequences of using state tests to promote students and evaluate schools," a letter in which she promised the education our students receive there "cannot be measured by a single test score."

The New Culture of Testing

And the next day, the faculty shepherded the entire student body into the gym to cheer for the students to "Do your best" and sing, to the tune of "Ghostbusters," that they were "test crushers."

The rally may have been a well-intentioned attempt to defuse students' pre-test jitters. A school administrator later told me, "It wasn't to further promote testing. It was just about increasing confidence." Our principal echoed the sentiment, saying, "We did a very intense test prep this year. We recognize that our kids were saturated and starting to feel overload. The kids seemed like they needed to let loose." And, she noted, "The idea of bringing a group together to garner enthusiasm is something we do all the time."

But the ultimate effect had a strangely *Hunger Games* tang to it—a mood of forced, rah-rah reassurance to the terrified children going into the arena, cheered on by those too young to yet participate.

Unnervingly, it was a scene being played out in other schools all around the country, as they too have prepared their students for a series of tests many have been practicing for since September. The night of the rally, I spoke to my schoolteacher friend Blair in Pennsylvania, who told me they'd done similar events at her school and both of her sons' schools, complete with near-identical catchy songs and even merchandise giveaways.

"They sang 'I will do my best best best' to the tune of 'Dynamite.' It would have been cute if it wasn't evil," she said. "They hang up banners in the schools that say 'I will do my best on the test.' We get robocalled from all three schools before the test days. It's all almost exactly the same wording from each principal. It's a disgrace." Next year, up to half of her salary will be tied to how her students performed on their tests, a system that puts teachers who work with English learners or children with special needs—who might be great students but not great English language test takers—at risk for punitive measures.

The Impact of Testing on Education

But teachers are far from the only ones who feel the effects of the high-stakes testing game. My high school teacher friend Ariel says, "My honors English curriculum now contains only two books, instead of the 12 I used to teach. And very few short stories. It's mostly nonfiction, because that's what will be on the tests. Any books I teach outside of the curriculum will harm my students' scores on the tests that evaluate them and my performance. Goodbye, *Lord of the Flies*. Goodbye, *Macbeth*. Goodbye, *A Separate Peace*. Most good teachers are demoralized by the test, and horrified by what it is doing to education."

Meanwhile, Paula, an elementary school art teacher and mother of two, tells me the tests take a big bite out of what used to be legitimate learning time. "My classes are directly affected. My curriculum is affected. My classes are cancelled for test prep and they are not made up," she says. "This afternoon I was told that I must remove all the student art work hanging in the room, as it 'will be a distraction to the students taking the tests.'"

And, she says, it's changing the way students view their education. "Children are getting the message at a very young age that if you pick the right choice between several options you can be successful. That's not the way to learn, especially creatively. That's not experimenting or exploring or creating. We're telling kids that life is a series of hoops and that they need to start jumping through them very early."

Meanwhile, teachers and principals are caught in a hideous bind of having their own teaching methods squeezed out while knowing that, as Paula says, "Millions of dollars of funding and aid for students they genuinely care about are tied up in these test outcomes." Schools that score poorly on the tests wind up slated for closure or downsizing. Is it any wonder that administrators find themselves drawn to acts of intimidation and cheating? No wonder, too, that New York teacher Gerald "Jerry" Conti went viral earlier this month when he wrote a letter of resignation in which he spoke for plenty of other educators, lamenting, "'Data driven' education seeks only conformity, standardization, testing and a zombie-like adherence to the shallow and generic Common Core, along with a lockstep of oversimplified so-called Essential Learnings. Creativity, academic freedom, teacher autonomy, experimentation and innovation are being stifled. . . . In their pursuit of federal tax dollars, our legislators have failed us by selling children out to private industries such as Pearson Education. . . . I am not leaving my profession, in truth, it has left me."

And it's a system that, as core standards are being implemented around the country, seems built to fail. "All the passing ratings are going to go down about 30 percent this year; that's what they're predicting," says author, advocate and edu-

The History of Testing US Students

American schoolchildren have been taking achievement tests for decades. In the 1950s, they used their well-sharpened number 2 pencils on something called the Iowa Test of Basic Skills, which is still in use and is almost exclusively multiple-choice. Tests of this period were of the low-stakes variety—indeed, they usually weren't required at all—and they were "norm referenced," meaning that students were rated as they compared to each other. (Nancy was in the 90th percentile, Susie in the 70th, and so on.) When the Russians launched the Sputnik satellite in 1957, U.S. schools came under pressure to up their game. The Elementary and Secondary Education Act of 1965 (ESEA), the precursor to No Child Left Behind [Act], focused federal funding on poor schools with low-achieving students. Meanwhile, there was a growing feeling among the public that all students should be striving for well-defined learning goals and be tested on that basis. Some of this demand for data on students' achievement was met by the National Assessment of Educational Progress [NAEP], popularly known as the Nation's Report Card, which was first administered in 1969. The NAEP measured just a sampling of students, and it didn't break out state results as it does now, but it marked a trend toward using tests to monitor performance.

Susan Headden,
"A Test Worth Teaching To: The Race to Fix America's Broken System of Standardized Exams,"
Washington Monthly, *May/June 2012.*

cation historian Diane Ravitch. "The dark view is that they want everybody to fail and they want people to say the public schools stink, so they can push for more vouchers and more charters. I can't describe what's going on without thinking that we're in the process of destroying American public education."

A Poor Strategy for Improving Education

How'd we wind up in this mess? Ravitch says it started back in 2000 with [President] George W. Bush, and his so-called "Texas Miracle"—the promise that standardized testing had revolutionized his home state and closed the achievement gap. It's what led to the implementation of the No Child Left Behind [Act (NCLB)] when he became president, and [President Barack] Obama's subsequent Race to the Top—a program Ravitch describes as even "worse" than NCLB. And you've got to wonder, if Texas had truly been so miraculous, would it now be the epicenter of a powerful anti-testing backlash? Ravitch is not opposed to diagnostics—nor, for that matter, are any of the teachers I spoke with. She explains, "The test should be designed by the teachers, and kids should be tested based on what they're taught. Instead, the test makers are telling educators what to teach—and that's backwards. All of this is a terrible distortion of education." Or as my friend Blair puts it, "This is random. The test is created by somebody far away. It's very shallow and it doesn't measure higher order thinking."

My seventh- and third-grade daughters are both enrolled in wonderful public schools—schools that just happen to exist within a system in which children's academic opportunities, their teachers' careers, and the viability of their schools themselves increasingly boil down to six nail-biting, test-taking days in the spring. Which is, by any way you want to quantify it, insane. Ultimately, the only clear-cut winners in the high-stakes assessment game are publishers like Pearson [Education], which two years ago won a $32 million contract to write the tests.

Two years ago, educator Will Logan wrote that "a culture of schooling that feels the need to pump up students for test taking with chanting and dancing . . . makes me actually shudder as a parent." And he added, with great economy and perception, that "if all we want for our kids is to pass the test, we really don't need schools any longer." It should be obvious that if we have reached the point where kids are so anxious that their schools are pumping them full of canned *esprit de corps* [group morale] tactics, there's a real problem there. The solution isn't rallies and funny songs. It's looking directly at the source of that brutal, academic year–gobbling problem itself. And then doing things differently.

Absolutely, there are broken schools and faulty teachers who are failing our children every day. But building a better system of public education—an education to which every child in this country is entitled—takes creative and innovative approaches, tailored to individual communities. Learning is not a one-size-fits-all proposition. And our kids and our schools shouldn't have their whole futures riding on how well children can fill in little circles, to be scored by machines. As Blair says, "We are exchanging authentic, age-appropriate learning—real thinking learning—for test taking. It makes me want to scream."

VIEWPOINT 2

"The benefits of testing far outweigh any disadvantages."

Standardized Testing Is a Good Way to Measure Student Learning

Herbert J. Walberg

In the following viewpoint, Herbert J. Walberg argues that standardized testing in schools has many benefits and is supported by the vast majority of Americans. Walberg claims that there are several fallacies about standardized tests, including that they take too much time and money, detract from real learning, and affect students and teachers negatively. Walberg is a university scholar at the University of Illinois at Chicago, a distinguished visiting fellow at the Hoover Institution, and chairman of the board of directors of the Heartland Institute.

As you read, consider the following questions:

1. According to the author, national surveys found that what fraction of high school students said schools should promote only individuals who master the material?

Herbert J. Walberg, "Higher Marks," *Hoover Digest*, October 12, 2011.

2. Walberg contends that in national surveys what percentage of faculty in colleges of education said they would like less reliance on multiple-choice examinations?

3. According to Walberg, tests sample as little as what percentage of all of the content and skills taught in school?

The American public supports high standards and testing. Parents want to know how well their children are doing academically—compared with other children their age, and in light of school standards. Taxpayers want to know if the money they pay for public schools is well spent. They would like to be assured that today's youth are getting the education they need to attain the prosperity of earlier generations.

Over the past four decades, more than two hundred public opinion polls compiled by Richard Phelps have consistently shown that the public strongly supports standardized tests. A high percentage of respondents endorse their use to measure educational goals and ensure that high school graduates have acquired the knowledge and skills they need for further education and adult life.

In another study, when respondents were asked to identify the top priorities for 2010, 65 percent of the public named education. Such findings offer strong evidence that the public is in favor of raising standards for American schools and using standardized tests to measure student and teacher progress.

Moreover, although educators might suggest that students are intimidated or anxious about taking standardized tests, strong evidence suggests that students prefer academic rigor. Many agree with the views that schools are lax, should raise their standards, and could do a better job holding students accountable for their performance. As revealed by national surveys, three-fourths of high school students believe that stiffer examination and graduation requirements would make students pay more attention to their studies. Students agree with research findings that suggest these accountability measures raise achievement levels.

Students want to receive credit for their academic efforts. They feel that their achievements would be tainted if diplomas were granted to unqualified students. In a random sample of high school students, three-fourths of the respondents said schools should promote only individuals who master the material. Standardized tests, of course, would be necessary for objective, efficient assessments of such mastery.

Students also offered reasonable advice for how they might attain such mastery. Nearly 67 percent of the respondents said students would learn more if they tried harder. About eight in ten respondents said students would learn more if schools made sure everyone was on time and completed all the homework. More than seven in ten said schools should require after-school classes for anyone earning Ds or Fs.

Students are not recommending that educational standards be lowered or that standardized testing programs be eliminated. They seem to understand the importance of their own and others' learning.

Educators Are Unmoved by the Benefits

American educators are among the most severe critics of standards and testing programs. Even amid poor test outcomes, they maintain that public schools have high standards and are delivering acceptable academic results. For example, in response to the statement "the school has high academic standards," seven in ten principals and six in ten teachers agreed. Yet only four in ten students were convinced that high standards were being upheld in their school.

When considering the statement "the classes are challenging," seven in ten principals and five in ten teachers agreed, but only two in ten students held such positive beliefs about their educational experiences. Their views obviously differ greatly from those of the public and students.

Similarly, education professors, who prepare aspiring and current teachers and administrators, report opinions sharply different from those of the public and students. In national surveys, 78 percent of the faculty in colleges of education said they would like to see less reliance on multiple-choice examinations. Only 24 percent believed it is "absolutely essential" to produce "teachers who understand how to work with the states' standards, tests, and accountability systems."

Their course outlines, reading assignments, and grading rubrics show indifference and even hostility toward using specific course objectives and measuring student outcomes. Despite the vast literature on the benefits of testing on learning, educators and especially the "educators of educators" generally do not support testing and standards. Their attitude aligns with some of the commonly held fallacies about standardized testing, which will be cited in a moment.

The benefits of testing far outweigh any disadvantages. Largely ignored by test critics and some educators are hundreds of well-designed studies, complete with comparison groups, showing these benefits. This voluminous research has been conveniently compiled in reviews of the research literature and statistical analysis of findings across multiple studies ("meta-analysis"). The conclusions are as follows:

- Setting unambiguous goals and measuring progress substantially increase student motivation and performance in learning, sports, and work settings.
- In K–12 and college classes, testing as often as weekly or daily promotes frequent preparation, which leads to increased learning. (Teaching students to frequently assess their own progress is an ultimate goal.)
- Giving students detailed test results helps them spot their weaknesses, increases their learning, and reduces the potential for overconfidence.
- Learning is reinforced and enhanced by offering students details on what they have done well.

- Using tests to verify that students have mastered or nearly mastered specific content before introducing new material yields better results than teaching that ignores students' mastery levels.
- When studies focus on language learning, frequent testing has intensified and increased the speed with which students learn new languages.

In addition to the comparison-group studies largely by psychologists, large, statistically controlled studies of states and nations show that on average, students who are required to pass standards- or curriculum-based examinations perform better than students who do not.

Such tests cover uniform subject matter in humanities, sciences, and other fields. The tests are graded by educators other than the students' own teachers, and students have little incentive to challenge their teachers about course content and standards. Rather, the students and teachers work together toward their joint goal of meeting standards, and often the stakes are high: graduation and university admission. Because the exams and courses are uniform, teachers can concentrate on how to teach—not what to teach. Knowing the subject matter in previous grades, teachers build upon what students have previously been taught.

Given all these findings, the benefits of testing appear to be as well established empirically as any principle in the social sciences.

In 2003, Ludger Woessmann . . . carried out perhaps the largest and most sophisticated causal analysis of national achievement. Using data from thirty-nine countries that participated in the Third International Mathematics and Science Study, he found that students in rich and poor nations learned the most when their countries employed external, curriculum-based examinations.

Six Fallacies About Standardized Tests

Gregory Cizek, writing in *Defending Standardized Testing*, points out several frequent but fallacious criticisms of standardized tests. Despite their lack of foundation, these ideas are repeated so often that they deserve to be considered and rebutted.

Fallacy number one: Testing consumes valuable time that would otherwise be used for instruction.

Testing is part of instruction, not separate from it. Lectures, discussion activities, and assigned readings are useful. However, teachers must determine if the students have actually learned course material and proceed accordingly to reteach or move on. Frequent, even daily, testing encourages students to be prepared for each class rather than "cramming" easily forgotten information after infrequent tests. When tests match curricular standards, they reinforce students' learning by requiring them to think through and practice material they have completely or partially learned.

Two comparative studies conducted by John Bishop of Cornell University provide evidence of the instructional value of standardized tests. In one study, Bishop found that countries requiring students to take nationally standardized tests showed higher test scores on international tests than students in countries not requiring such tests.

In a second study, Bishop found that U.S. students who anticipated having to pass an examination for high school graduation learned more science and math, were more likely to complete homework and talk with their parents about schoolwork, and watched less television than their peers who were not required to pass such exams. Students concentrated on meeting standards and monitoring their own time and progress—skills important for not only increased achievement but also increased success in life.

Fallacy number two: Testing programs consume sizable financial resources that would otherwise be used for instruction.

Standardized tests are not only effective but cost-efficient. They represent only a minuscule percentage of K–12 expenditures. Hoover [Institution] senior fellow Caroline Hoxby found that in 2000, $234 million went to commercial firms for services including standardized testing, standards setting, and accountability reporting. This amount was less than 0.1 percent of total spending on K–12 education and amounted to an average of only $5.81 per student. Across the twenty-five states with available information, the total cost per student was between $1.79 and $34.02.

It is true, however, that states and school districts have paid steadily and substantially more over the past decade to devise their own tests. But lacking test and testing expertise, they have poor records of test effectiveness and cost-efficiency. Backed by long records of experience and success in the marketplace, commercial tests are more objective and reliable than the tests that states and smaller localities have commissioned.

In addition, well-made commercial tests can yield excellent diagnostic results in improving achievement by identifying student strengths and weaknesses. Commercial tests, moreover, are increasingly administered by computer, and their costs can be expected to continue declining.

Fallacy number three: Content not covered by tests is neglected.

It is true that holding educators accountable for only mathematics and language arts may lead them to neglect history and science. But this point is an argument for comprehensive and systematic testing across the entire curriculum. Responsible test makers, moreover, do not purport to cover all the material students are expected to learn. Tests sample only a small fraction, perhaps as little as 5–10 percent, of all the content and skills.

Just as a national survey may interview a few tenths of a percent of the population, a fifty-minute multiple-choice test of perhaps fifty items provides a good estimate of a student's overall achievement. Like a national survey designed to sample various parts of the country, moreover, a standardized test can sample the multiple topics students are expected to learn. Thus, such tests can sample far more content than a few essay questions.

Fallacy number four: Tests overemphasize factual knowledge and low-level skills.

Well-designed standardized tests can measure knowledge, understanding, application of ideas, and other high-level skills. Designers can use single items with a clear, correct answer to assess lower-level skills. They also can combine items and ask respondents to select the best answer when assessing complex knowledge. Tests assessing complex achievement require respondents to select the best idea from a group of different and compelling positions and require respondents to identify the best reason for action, the best interpretation of a set of ideas, or the best application of important principles. (Rather than the word "correct," "best" is advisable because more than one answer may be correct to some degree.)

Whereas tests emphasizing single, correct answers are common for students in early grades or who are new to an area of study, a wider range of items requiring interpretation is found on more advanced tests. K–12 students who practice demonstrating their knowledge and skills on standardized tests throughout their school career become better prepared to meet future educational, occupational, and professional goals. They are ready for the standardized tests used for admission to selective colleges and graduate and professional schools. In addition, K–12 students are prepared for tests required for occupational licensing for trades as well as for intellectually demanding professions such as law and medicine.

Fallacy number five: Testing places excessive pressure on students.

The world outside school is demanding. The knowledge economy increasingly demands more knowledge and higher skills of workers, requiring larger amounts of intense study of difficult subjects. Yet American students spend only about half the total study time of Asian students in regular schools, in tutoring schools, and on homework. Thus, some pressure is advisable for the future welfare of the students and the nation.

When students can see their progress toward standards, they may find that incremental progress motivates them and pressure is more manageable. Practice enhances their performance, as in games and sports. Testing programs allow educators to accommodate their curriculums to better meet the needs of students with different achievement levels, giving special help to those who fall behind and accelerating or enriching learning for advanced students.

Fallacy number six: Testing fosters malaise among all teachers.

Good schools focus on student learning, not on the satisfaction of the professional staff. If data show that testing benefits students, it should be pursued even if teachers decline to offer unanimous support. But professionals should take pride in seeing good results from their work—and because testing reveals good work and aids rather than detracts from instruction, teachers should embrace it.

Many teachers are unfamiliar with why testing is necessary and how good tests are designed and administered. Often, a teacher's opposition is based on an experience in which the test was poorly designed, not aligned with the curriculum, or in some other way incorrectly administered. Professional development programs that include guidance on how to align classroom activities with achievement standards are one solution. Teachers can also learn to see the shortcomings of tests they designed, and thus how to devise better tests.

Good student performance on tests should be a source of satisfaction for teachers. For schools as a whole, the appropriate tests are a reliable gauge of strengths and weaknesses, pointing the way toward improvements in curriculum, teaching, and learning.

VIEWPOINT 3

> *"The fixation on testing is putting undue stress on educators as well as students, and, in many instances, punishing teachers and schools."*

Disappearing Act: End the Testing Fixation Before It Erases More Meaningful Education

Virginia Myers

In the following viewpoint, Virginia Myers argues that high-stakes testing that now occurs in schools is having negative effects on teachers and students. Myers contends that teachers report undue stress and time taken away from the content they believe they should be teaching. She claims that students are under too much stress from the testing, which fails to take into account mitigating factors that affect student and school performance. In addition, she claims that the way testing is currently implemented fails as an adequate tool of assessment. Myers writes for the American Federation of Teachers [AFT].

Virginia Myers, "Disappearing Act: End the Testing Fixation Before It Erases More Meaningful Education," *American Teacher*, March/April 2013, pp. 12–13.

As you read, consider the following questions:

1. The author claims that in Chicago, children as young as what age are being given standardized tests?
2. According to Myers, Florida teachers report that how many school days a year have some form of testing?
3. What factors does Myers identify that may skew test results?

When it comes to testing, teachers, parents and even some students agree on one thing: They have had about all they can take. And for good reason. The fixation on testing is putting undue stress on educators as well as students, and, in many instances, punishing teachers and schools. It's also short-changing vital parts of the curriculum, including arts, music and physical education.

Bonnie Cunard, who teaches eighth-grade language arts in Fort Myers, Fla., feels the pinch in her classroom, sacrificing hours to test preparation and administration. For seven of the 10 months in the school year, the entire language arts curriculum revolves around the writing portion of standardized tests, says Cunard, a member of the Teachers' Association of Lee County. Students sacrifice time they could spend studying literature to practice persuasive and expository writing, because if they don't do well the school could lose its Title I status and the corresponding resources it needs to serve these children.

The system destroys holistic learning, says Cunard, noting also that it adds a lot of pressure. "The school is depending on me for the writing scores." Meanwhile, her personal evaluations (based on the value-added model) depend on reading scores—and she doesn't even teach reading; that's another teacher's responsibility. "It's frustrating," says Cunard. "I feel like I have no control."

In Chicago, children as young as 4 are lining up for multiple standardized tests. "We're doing it to our babies," protests preschool teacher Kristen Roberts. Chicago preschoolers face a test called the Kindergarten Readiness Tool before they even enter elementary school; kindergartners endure 14 different standardized tests in one year. "I find it very demoralizing," says Roberts. "Testing young children is developmentally inappropriate. This is damaging to teaching and to learning."

Many parents agree.

The Pressure's On

Amy Green's daughter, a third grader, comes home close to tears on test days: Despite teacher assurance that the child might not know many of the answers, the tests make her "feel stupid." For that reason, Green is keeping her younger son out of public schools and will enroll him in a private kindergarten instead. "I won't subject him to 14 tests that are going to absolutely kill his self-esteem about who he is as a learner."

Older students feel the stress, too. Members of Voices of Youth in Chicago Education (VOYCE) joined the Chicago Teachers Union [CTU] to protest over-testing, carrying chains of more than 12,000 pencils strung together to represent the number of hours students lose to standardized testing in a single year. In addition to swallowing up precious learning time as teachers teach to the test, too many tests are closely tied to school and teacher evaluations. Students object to this. "Our test scores should not be used to jeopardize our teachers' careers," high school junior Victor Alquicira told a large CTU rally last September. Quoted in the *Chicago Sun-Times*, he added, "It's not fair to judge teachers on student test scores when there [are] so many factors beyond their control."

Those sorts of factors can severely affect test scores on any given day, points out Philadelphia English teacher Bonnee Breese. At her high-poverty high school, students may arrive on test days with any number of personal crises that prevent them from performing well. Some are homeless, bouncing from homeless shelters to makeshift arrangements with relatives and friends. Others have parents who are largely unavailable to care for them and their siblings. "Sometimes there has been some sort of traumatic violence in their lives the night before the test, and they come in the next day because school is the only place they had to come," says Breese, a member of the Philadelphia Federation of Teachers. She's even had students attend school on testing days when "they couldn't keep their heads up off the desk and stop crying because a parent had died the night before."

In New York City, some parents are boycotting test days. "I want my school to use tests to help instruction, to help find out if kids don't know fractions," parent Lori Chajet told the *New York Times*. "I don't want my child to feel like her score will decide if her teacher has a job or not." Chajet kept her daughter home from school to protest a test designed to choose which questions should be included on future state exams.

"We believe education should focus on developing the imagination of a child, not on putting them through stressful and mind-numbing standardized tests, day after day," reads the website for New York's Parent Voices, an advocacy group against high-stakes testing. "We are here to say: Enough is enough!"

Research shows how extreme the testing culture has become. A superintendent in Monroe County, N.Y., testified that in the first two months of school, more than 20,000 pretests were administered to 4,000 students; Florida teachers say their schools have some form of testing 80–90 school days a year; and in Texas, up to 45 days each school year are spent on testing activities.

A Tool That Doesn't Work

Many who follow education policy assert that intensive testing does not help students advance. In fact, some studies show that more students drop out when faced with an exit exam,

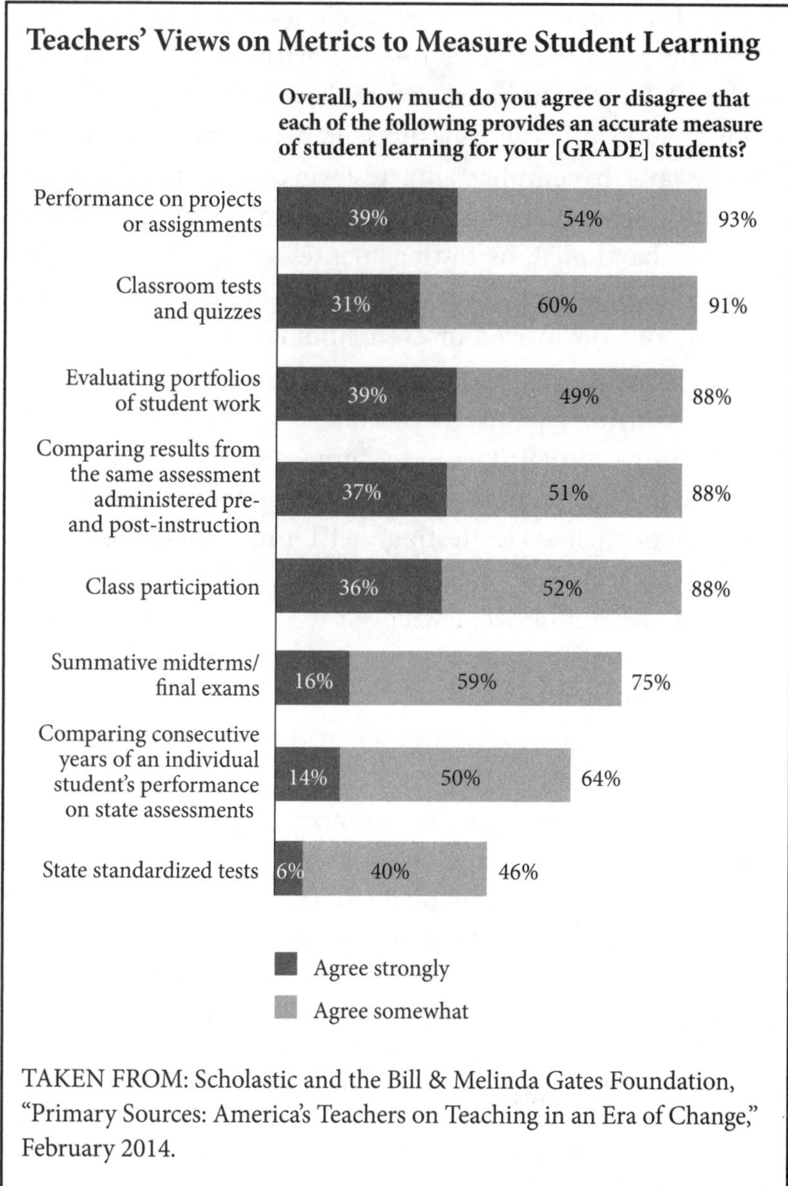

TAKEN FROM: Scholastic and the Bill & Melinda Gates Foundation, "Primary Sources: America's Teachers on Teaching in an Era of Change," February 2014.

which they must pass to graduate from high school. That would be the opposite of our goal: to educate every student.

Too many tests can erode the quality of education for students who stay in school as well: Teachers feel compelled to produce high scores, to protect their jobs and to keep their schools open, so they focus on rote learning and memorization, test-taking techniques and shallow approaches to material that could otherwise be presented in more creative, enriching ways. By emphasizing test success, critical-thinking skills and deeper learning are ignored. In fact, entire subject areas are abandoned, as testing focuses primarily on English and math. Science, music, art and physical education are often lost, programs downsized or even eliminated.

This is not to say that all testing is detrimental. But as the AFT's resolution against high-stakes testing states, testing should inform, not impede, teaching and learning. "Public education should be obsessed with high-quality teaching and learning, not high-stakes testing," AFT president Randi Weingarten says. "Tests have a role to play, but today's fixation with them is undermining what we need to do to give kids a challenging and well-rounded education and to fairly measure teachers' performance."

Testing is particularly problematic when it becomes the sole determinant of success—or failure. When many factors can skew test results—student absences, large numbers of English language learners, and the personal traumas and stresses that may influence an individual student's ability to focus on a test day—the tests need to be supplemented with other measures. Classroom observation, student portfolios and performance-based assessment are some options.

Equity and Fairness

The accepted intention of testing is to improve performance for all students, in all schools. But many would argue that the opposite is true. When poor test scores result in school closings, tests can take away the very institutions our neediest students rely upon to improve: their neighborhood schools.

"There's a huge impact," says Monique Redoe, a member of the Chicago Teachers Union, cochair of the Chicago black teachers' caucus, and a seventh- and eighth-grade social studies teacher. "We know we have biased tests," she explains, citing the subjective nature of creating test questions that reflect the cultural background of the majority population, and not the life experience of minorities. The result: Low-income, minority students fail at disproportionate rates. "Because of that," she says, "8 percent of the school closures have been in black communities."

Once those public schools close, private schools move in. "I believe testing is a weapon," says Redoe. "It's being used as a weapon to privatize education."

Viewpoint 4

> *"The [Tennessee Education Association's] campaign highlights the need for testing data to be used more carefully and demonstrates the power of teachers to act effectively when it is not."*

Evaluating Teachers by Student Test Scores Can Be Arbitrary

Molly Rusk

In the following viewpoint, Molly Rusk argues that a recent campaign by Tennessee teachers to get rid of a law tying teacher licensing decisions to test scores was rightly opposed. Rusk contends that the assessment tool in Tennessee was unreliable and unfairly punished teachers who teach at challenging schools with lower-performing students. She claims that by educating the legislature, the teachers were able to eliminate the assessment tool, providing an example for teachers' unions around the country. Rusk is a writer for Yes! *magazine.*

Molly Rusk, "Tennessee Tied Teachers' Jobs to Standardized Test Scores. Here's How They Pushed Back—And Won," *Yes!*, May 30, 2014.

As you read, consider the following questions:

1. In what year did Tennessee adopt the Tennessee Value-Added Assessment System (TVAAS), according to the author?
2. According to Rusk, what percentage of the score for evaluating teachers came from TVAAS after implementation of Race to the Top in 2010?
3. According to the author, how many people signed a petition asking the Tennessee governor to treat teachers as professionals?

What if a surgeon's medical license could be taken away based on an error-prone statistical formula that ranked his abilities on a scale of 1 to 5, based on the success (or failure) of a small number of the operations he performed? Or imagine if a lawyer could lose her membership to the bar because a statistical estimate of her success predicted that she would lose the majority of her cases next year.

A Campaign Against a Teacher Evaluation Tool

Last year [2013], public school teachers in Tennessee faced precisely that situation, but they didn't take it lying down. Instead, they started a year of creative actions that led to a decisive change in policy—despite a governor determined to keep an unreliable statistical formula as a key method of evaluating teachers.

Their campaign ended successfully on April 24 [2014], when Governor Bill Haslam signed a bill rolling back the use of a statistical instrument known as TVAAS [Tennessee Value-Added Assessment System] in teacher licensing decisions—and hitting the pause button on an important facet of the testing trend in Tennessee, at least for the moment.

Education experts are divided as to what this development will mean for America's schoolkids. But many believe that it could spark similar campaigns nationwide.

"The change in Tennessee sends a message about politics," said Dan Goldhaber, director of the Center for Education Data and Research at the University of Washington. "It will embolden people in other states who think that tests ought not to be used for teacher evaluations to continue the push-back."

According to Bob Peterson, president of the Milwaukee teachers' union, the development in Tennessee is just one piece of the puzzle. "The success of the pushback in Tennessee is one part of the larger growing movement for testing reform, against the use of standardized tests to pigeonhole and sort our students, and to scapegoat our public schools and teachers," Peterson said. "New York, California, Oregon—there's growing grassroots activity."

A Statistical Tool

The story begins in the early 1990s, when the state of Tennessee hired Dr. Bill Sanders, then a statistician at the University of Tennessee's program in agriculture, to develop a statistical tool that could measure how well teachers were doing their jobs. So Sanders created the Tennessee Value-Added Assessment System.

Also known as TVAAS, the state adopted the system in 1993, and school district administrators and board members used it as a diagnostic of how schools and teachers were performing.

While Sanders was a perfectly good statistician, some have cracked wise about his background. "His initial forays into statistical modeling were based on livestock—chickens and cows," said Jim Wrye, manager of government relations for the Tennessee Education Association [TEA], the largest professional association of teachers in the state.

In the context of increasing federal pressure to emphasize testing in public schools, TVAAS was seen as a limited tool. It gathered information about how a given teacher's students were doing on the state's standardized test and spat out a number from 1 to 5, with 5 being best. It showed in a general way how well teachers were preparing students for the test. Soon other states began adopting systems based on TVAAS.

But then, beginning in 2010, Tennessee made several policy decisions that changed the role TVAAS played in teachers' lives.

A Competition for Education Funding

The reason for the change was a federal initiative called Race to the Top, introduced in 2010, which put states in competition for education funding. The states that came up with the best education reform plans—defined by a set of goals laid out by the federal government—would win a large public education grant. Among the goals of Race to the Top was teacher accountability. To meet that goal, United States secretary of education Arne Duncan encouraged school districts to use student test scores to decide whether teachers could receive or renew their teaching licenses, among other things.

In order to win Race to the Top funding—the state was awarded more than $501 million—Tennessee turned TVAAS scores into a major component of teacher evaluations. While 51 percent of a teacher's total score still came from an observation—in which a school district official would visit a school and watch a teacher in action—TVAAS scores were now worth 35 percent.

In August 2013, the State Board of Education voted to adopt a policy, introduced by state education commissioner Kevin Huffman, which placed even more weight on TVAAS scores. Under this new policy, if a teacher scored lower than 2 out of 5 points for three years in a row, she would not be eligible to renew her license.

Before that decision, TVAAS scores didn't cause much trouble because they were only a diagnostic, with no real consequences. But when teachers realized that these erratic scores could put their careers on the line, they started getting worried.

"The most valuable possession of a teacher is her license," Wrye said. "A license allows her to do what she loves. It's worth more than her house, it's worth more than her car. And when you decide to take it away, you better have rock-solid reason."

Teacher Complaints About the System

Teachers saw TVAAS as anything but rock-solid. Like other statistical measurements, it has what's known as a "standard error." In other words, a teacher could receive a score of 5 for a given school year but actually deserve only a 3, according to other components of her evaluation. By the same token, a teacher could receive 3 points for a given year, but actually deserve a 5. Errors of this nature are built into statistics, but the likelihood that this would occur was relatively high for TVAAS.

The system was so unpredictable, said Wrye, "It was sometimes viewed as the crazy aunt in the basement."

Wrye also said the system unfairly punished teachers who work in the neediest communities. "Places with high poverty, places with low resources, places that have a high influx of English language learners—there are places where, no matter what the teacher does, they will not have very good test scores or TVAAS scores."

Last year, complaints about TVAAS began trickling in to the TEA. As the association investigated individual cases, they discovered how the system's standard error, among other kinks, was affecting teachers, according to TEA president Gera Summerford. In one instance, eighth-grade teacher Mark Taylor was denied a bonus because of poor scores, even though the scores only reflected the work of about 16 percent of his students.

Public Opinion on Teacher Evaluations

Some states require that teacher evaluations include how well a teacher's students perform on standardized tests. Do you favor or oppose this requirement?

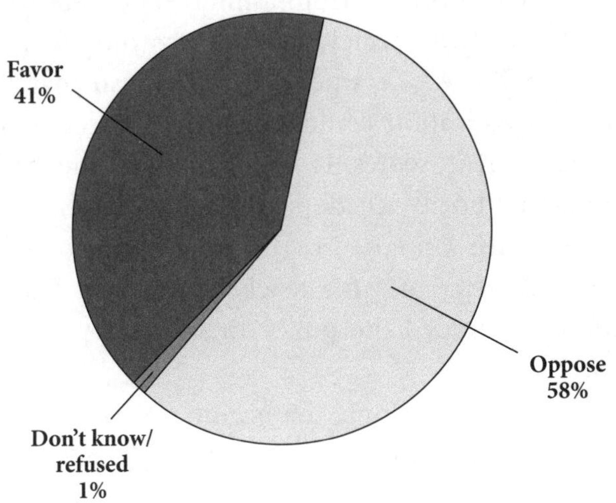

TAKEN FROM: Phi Delta Kappa International (PDK)/Gallup poll, May 2013.

These kinds of complaints made it clear that the August 2013 decision—set to take effect in 2015—could cost a teacher her license and perhaps her whole career because of an erratic and often inaccurate statistical calculation. So the TEA launched a campaign to urge the Tennessee legislature to reverse the policy and ensure fairness in teacher evaluations.

An Education for the Legislature

The TEA started by doing what teachers do best: educating. "What we ended up doing is, first and foremost, explaining to the legislature what exactly TVAAS was," said Jim Wrye, who was among the TEA leaders who spearheaded the campaign.

On January 23, two TEA allies, Senator Mike Bell and House Rep. Matthew Hill, presented an initial bill, the Educator Respect and Accountability Act of 2014, that would completely remove student standardized test scores from teacher evaluations.

But because of pressure from a minority of legislators who supported the existing policy, the bill was modified to focus specifically on TVAAS. It amended the law so that the state department of education could not revoke a teacher's license based on her TVAAS scores. It also took away the state board of education's authority to adopt policies on teacher licensing.

Meanwhile, on January 31, the state board of education met to finalize new rules for teachers' licenses. During that meeting, they rescinded the policy they had approved in August 2013.

But that reversal was only the beginning. The modified bill still had to survive a gauntlet of committees, subcommittees, and hearings.

On February 4, Jim Wrye and TEA general counsel Rick Colbert gave a 15 minute presentation before the state's House education committee, laying out the major problems with TVAAS. Other TEA leaders gave a similar presentation for the Senate education committee.

Once members of the legislature understood that TVAAS was not a state standardized test but rather an unreliable statistical estimate derived from standardized test scores, the bill gained widespread support. Within two weeks, 88 out of 99 members of the Tennessee legislature, including both House representatives and senators, signed on as cosponsors.

A Policy Victory

Despite the growing support for a policy change in the legislature and in the State Board of Education, the governor was determined to keep TVAAS as a core component of teacher evaluations. Tennessee education commissioner Kevin Huffman was the leading proponent of this policy, and Governor Haslam personally lobbied senators, urging them to support the commissioner's position.

"One senator said he had spent over 10 years in the general assembly and [had] never been called to the governor's office on a particular bill, before this one," Wrye said. "He still voted for us in committee."

The TEA leaders didn't do all the talking. The association organized more than 400 teachers who went to Nashville during spring break to personally talk to legislators about TVAAS and other public education issues like charter schools and vouchers.

The TEA also created a petition asking the governor to treat teachers as professionals. After nearly 12,000 people signed the petition, the TEA delivered it to Governor Haslam's office with comments outlining the key reasons that the TEA's licensure bill had gained such widespread support in the legislature.

The final twist of the screw came in the form of two lawsuits that the TEA filed against Governor Haslam and Commissioner Huffman. The lawsuits were based on separate complaints that two teachers—one of whom was eighth-grade teacher Mark Taylor, mentioned above—had brought to the association about TVAAS. In both cases, the teachers lost bonuses they believed they deserved, due to poor TVAAS scores that did not represent the full extent of their work.

TEA president Summerford stressed that the lawsuits did not address teacher licensure rules, the issue at the heart of the association's licensure bill.

However, they "bring into sharp focus . . . the fundamental flaws of TVAAS in making high-stakes decisions for teachers," Wrye said.

In the end, there were only six "no" votes on the TEA's licensure bill in the Tennessee legislature, out of a total of 132 voting members. And when Governor Haslam signed the bill on April 24, teachers across the state celebrated the development as a major policy victory.

"It showed tremendous care and support by the rank-and-file senators and House members for their teachers," said Wrye.

Federal pressure to emphasize testing in public schools will continue to affect education policy in Tennessee and in the rest of the country. But the TEA's campaign highlights the need for testing data to be used more carefully and demonstrates the power of teachers to act effectively when it is not.

Viewpoint 5

> *"Even in very diverse classes, kids tend to agree about what they see happening day after day."*

Students Should Evaluate Their Teachers

Amanda Ripley

In the following viewpoint, Amanda Ripley argues that recent research on the use of student evaluations of teachers illustrates that students should have a role to play in teacher assessment. Ripley claims that when student surveys are done well—asking the right questions—the results are surprisingly consistent and informative. She suggests that such assessments may be reliable enough to be used as a key component in making decisions about teacher salaries and promotions. Ripley is a journalist and the author of The Smartest Kids in the World—and How They Got That Way.

As you read, consider the following questions:

1. Ripley reports that at the beginning of 2012, approximately what fraction of the states required teacher evaluations to be at least partially based on test-score data?

Amanda Ripley, "Why Kids Should Grade Teachers," *Atlantic*, October 2012. www.theatlantic.com.

2. The author claims that the Bill and Melinda Gates Foundation found that students' responses to what five statements were most correlated with student learning?

3. Ripley claims that the best evidence concerning student surveys comes from where?

In towns around the country this past school year [2011–2012], a quarter-million students took a special survey designed to capture what they thought of their teachers and their classroom culture. Unlike the vast majority of surveys in human history, this one had been carefully field-tested. That research had shown something remarkable: If you asked kids the right questions, they could identify, with uncanny accuracy, their most—and least—effective teachers.

The point was so obvious, it was almost embarrassing. Kids stared at their teachers for hundreds of hours a year, which might explain their expertise. Their survey answers, it turned out, were more reliable than any other known measure of teacher performance—including classroom observations and student test-score growth. All of which raised an uncomfortable new question: Should teachers be paid, trained, or dismissed based in part on what children say about them?

To find out, school officials in a handful of cities have been quietly trying out the survey. In D.C. this year, six schools participated in a pilot project, and the *Atlantic* was granted access to observe the four-month process from beginning to end. . . .

Concern About Teaching Quality

For the past decade, education reformers worldwide have been obsessed with teaching quality. Study after study has shown that it matters more than anything else in a school—and that it is too low in too many places. For all kids to learn 21st-century skills, teaching has to get better—somehow.

In the United States, the strategy has been for school officials to start evaluating teacher performance more frequently and more seriously than in the past, when their reviews were almost invariably positive. The hope was that a teacher would improve through a combination of pressure and feedback—or get replaced by someone better. By the beginning of this year, almost half the states required teacher reviews to be based in part on test-score data.

So far, this revolution has been loud but unsatisfying. Most teachers do not consider test-score data a fair measure of what students have learned. Complex algorithms that adjust for students' income and race have made test-score assessments more fair—but are widely resented, contested, or misunderstood by teachers.

Meanwhile, the whole debate remains moot in most classrooms. Despite all the testing in American schools, most teachers still do not teach the subjects or grade levels covered by mandatory standardized tests. So no test-score data exists upon which they can be judged. As a result, they still get evaluated by their principals, who visit their classrooms every so often and judge their work just as principals have always done—without much accuracy, detail, or candor. Even in Washington, D.C., which has been more aggressive than any other city in using test-score data to reward and fire teachers, such data have been collected for only 15 out of every 100 teachers. The proportion is increasing in D.C. public schools and other districts as schools pile on more tests, but for now, only a minority of teachers can be evaluated this way.

But even if testing data existed for everyone, how informative would they really be? Test scores can reveal when kids are not learning; they can't reveal *why*. They might make teachers relax or despair—but they can't help teachers improve. The surveys focus on the means, not the ends—giving teachers tangible ideas about what they can fix right now, straight from the minds of the people who sit in front of them all day long.

The Importance of Teachers

A decade ago, a Harvard economist named Ronald Ferguson went to Ohio to help a small school district figure out why black kids did worse on tests than white kids. He did all kinds of things to analyze the schoolchildren in Shaker Heights, a Cleveland suburb. Maybe because he'd grown up in the area, or maybe because he is African American himself, he suspected that important forces were at work in the classroom that teachers could not see.

So eventually Ferguson gave the kids in Shaker Heights a survey—not about their entire school, but about their specific classrooms. The results were counterintuitive. The same group of kids answered differently from one classroom to the next, but the differences didn't have as much to do with race as he'd expected; in fact, black students and white students largely agreed.

The variance had to do with the teachers. In one classroom, kids said they worked hard, paid attention, and corrected their mistakes; they liked being there, and they believed that the teacher cared about them. In the next classroom, the very same kids reported that the teacher had trouble explaining things and didn't notice when students failed to understand a lesson.

"We knew the relationships that teachers build with students were important," says Mark Freeman, superintendent of the Shaker Heights City School District. "But seeing proof of it in the survey results made a big difference. We found the results to be exceptionally helpful."

Back at Harvard, no one took much notice of Ferguson's survey. "When I would try to talk about it to my researcher colleagues, they were not interested," he says, laughing. "People would just change the subject."

A Research Study

Then, in 2009, the Bill and Melinda Gates Foundation launched a massive project to study 3,000 teachers in seven cities and learn what made them effective—or ineffective. Thomas Kane, a colleague of Ferguson's, led the sprawling study, called the "Measures of Effective Teaching" project. He and his fellow researchers set up many elaborate instruments to gauge effectiveness, including statistical regressions that tracked changes in students' test scores over time and panoramic video cameras that captured thousands of hours of classroom activity.

But Kane also wanted to include student perceptions. So he thought of Ferguson's survey, which he'd heard about at Harvard. With Ferguson's help, Kane and his colleagues gave an abbreviated version of the survey to the tens of thousands of students in the research study—and compared the results with test scores and other measures of effectiveness. The responses did indeed help predict which classes would have the most test-score improvement at the end of the year. In math, for example, the teachers rated most highly by students delivered the equivalent of about six more months of learning than teachers with the lowest ratings. (By comparison, teachers who get a master's degree—one of the few ways to earn a pay raise in most schools—delivered about one more month of learning per year than teachers without one.)

Students were better than trained adult observers at evaluating teachers. This wasn't because they were smarter but because they had months to form an opinion, as opposed to 30 minutes. And there were dozens of them, as opposed to a single principal. Even if one kid had a grudge against a teacher or just blew off the survey, his response alone couldn't sway the average.

"There are some students, knuckleheads who will just mess the survey up and not take it seriously," Ferguson says, "but they are very rare." Students who don't read the questions might give the same response to every item. But when Ferguson recently examined 199,000 surveys, he found that less than one-half of 1 percent of students did so in the first

10 questions. Kids, he believes, find the questions interesting, so they tend to pay attention. And the "right" answer is not always apparent, so even kids who want to skew the results would not necessarily know how to do it.

Even young children can evaluate their teachers with relative accuracy, to Kane's surprise. In fact, the only thing that the researchers found to better predict a teacher's test-score gains was . . . past test-score gains. But in addition to being loathed by teachers, those data are fickle. A teacher could be ranked as highly effective one year according to students' test gains and as ineffective the next, partly because of changes in class makeup that have little to do with her own performance—say, getting assigned the school's two biggest hooligans or meanest mean girls.

The Questions in the Survey

Student surveys, on the other hand, are far less volatile. Kids' answers for a given teacher remained similar, Ferguson found, from class to class and from fall to spring. And more important, the questions led to revelations that test scores did not: *Above and beyond academic skills, what was it really like to spend a year in this classroom? Did you work harder in this classroom than you did anywhere else?* The answers to these questions matter to a student for years to come, long after she forgets the quadratic equation.

The survey did not ask *Do you like your teacher? Is your teacher nice?* This wasn't a popularity contest. The survey mostly asked questions about what students saw, day in and day out.

Of the 36 items included in the Gates Foundation study, the five that most correlated with student learning were very straightforward:

1. *Students in this class treat the teacher with respect.*
2. *My classmates behave the way my teacher wants them to.*

3. *Our class stays busy and doesn't waste time.*

4. *In this class, we learn a lot almost every day.*

5. *In this class, we learn to correct our mistakes.*

When Ferguson and Kane shared these five statements at conferences, teachers were surprised. They had typically thought it most important to care about kids, but what mattered more, according to the study, was whether teachers had control over the classroom *and* made it a challenging place to be. As most of us remember from our own school days, those two conditions did not always coexist: some teachers had high levels of control, but low levels of rigor.

After the initial Gates findings came out, in 2010, Ferguson's survey gained statistical credibility. By then, the day-to-day work had been taken over by Cambridge Education, a for-profit consulting firm that helped school districts administer and analyze the survey. (Ferguson continues to receive a percentage of the profits from survey work.)

Student Surveys Across the Nation

Suddenly, dozens of school districts wanted to try out the survey, either through Cambridge or on their own—partly because of federal incentives to evaluate teachers more rigorously, using multiple metrics. This past school year, Memphis became the first school system in the country to tie survey results to teachers' annual reviews; surveys counted for 5 percent of a teacher's evaluation. And that proportion may go up in the future. (Another 35 percent of the evaluation was tied to how much students' test scores rose or fell, and 40 percent to classroom observations.) At the end of the year, some Memphis teachers were dismissed for low evaluation scores—but less than 2 percent of the faculty.

The New Teacher Project [TNTP], a national nonprofit based in Brooklyn that recruits and trains new teachers, last school year used student surveys to evaluate 460 of its 1,006 teachers. "The advent of student feedback in teacher evaluations is among the most significant developments for education reform in the last decade," says Timothy Daly, the organization's president and a former teacher.

In Pittsburgh, all students took the survey last school year. The teachers' union objects to any attempt to use the results in performance reviews, but education officials may do so anyway in the not-too-distant future. In Georgia, principals will consider student survey responses when they evaluate teachers this school year. In Chicago, starting in the fall of 2013, student survey results will count for 10 percent of a teacher's evaluation.

No one knows whether the survey data will become less reliable as the stakes rise. (Memphis schools are currently studying their surveys to check for such distortions, with results expected later this year.) Kane thinks surveys should count for 20 to 30 percent of a teacher's evaluations—enough for teachers and principals to take them seriously, but not enough to motivate teachers to pander to students or to cheat by, say, pressuring students to answer in a certain way.

Ferguson, for his part, is torn. He is wary of forcing anything on teachers—but he laments how rarely schools that try the surveys use the results in a systematic way to help teachers improve. On average over the past decade, only a third of teachers even clicked on the link sent to their e-mail in-boxes to see the results. Presumably, more would click if the results affected their pay. For now, Ferguson urges schools to conduct the survey multiple times before making it count toward performance reviews.

Student Surveys in Universities

As it happens, both Kane and Ferguson, like most university professors, are evaluated partly on student surveys. Their students' opinions factor into salary discussions and promotion reviews, and those opinions are available to anyone enrolled in the schools where they teach. "I think most of my colleagues take it seriously—because the institution does," Ferguson says. "Your desire not to be embarrassed definitely makes you pay attention."

Still, Ferguson dreads reading those course evaluations. The scrutiny makes him uncomfortable, he admits, even though it can be helpful. Last year, one student suggested that he use a PowerPoint presentation so that he didn't waste time writing material on the board. He took the advice, and it worked well. Some opinions, he flat out ignores. "They say you didn't talk about something," he says, "and you know you talked about it 10 times."

In fact, the best evidence for—and against—student surveys comes from their long history in universities. Decades of research indicate that the surveys are only as valuable as the questions they include, the care with which they are administered—and the professors' reactions to them. Some studies have shown that students do indeed learn more in classes whose instructors get higher ratings; others have shown that professors inflate grades to get good reviews. So far, grades don't seem to significantly influence responses to Ferguson's survey: Students who receive A's rate teachers only about 10 percent higher than D students do, on average.

The most refreshing aspect of Ferguson's survey might be that the results don't change dramatically depending on students' race or income. That is not the case with test data: Nationwide, scores reliably rise (to varying degrees) depending on how white and affluent a school is. With surveys, the only effect of income may be the opposite one: Some evidence shows that kids with the most-educated parents give slightly *lower* scores to their teachers than their classmates do. Students' expectations seemingly rise along with their family income (a phenomenon also seen in patient surveys in the health care field). But overall, even in very diverse classes, kids tend to agree about what they see happening day after day.

Periodical and Internet Sources Bibliography

The following articles have been selected to supplement the diverse views presented in this chapter.

Thomas Ahn and Jacob Vigdor	"Were All Those Standardized Tests for Nothing?: The Lessons of No Child Left Behind," American Enterprise Institute, May 2013.
Tom DeWeese	"American Education Fails Because It Isn't Education," American Policy Center, April 11, 2011.
Kevin Drum	"The Kids Are All Right: Students Today Score Better on Tests than You Did," *Mother Jones*, September/October 2012.
Elise Grafe	"Sub-Standardized Testing," *World*, August 22, 2013.
Susan Headden	"A Test Worth Teaching To: The Race to Fix America's Broken System of Standardized Exams," *Washington Monthly*, May/June 2012.
Nat Hentoff	"At Last, Parents Rebel Against Standardized Tests," Cato.org, May 9, 2012.
Jack Jennings	"Long-Term Gains in Minority Education: An Overlooked Success?," *Huffington Post*, May 8, 2011.
Daniel Luzer	"The Trouble with Those Standardized Tests: They're Never Good Enough," *College Guide* (blog)—*Washington Monthly*, March 18, 2013.
Abby Rapoport	"A Standardized Testing Revolt," *American Prospect*, January 10, 2013.
Diane Ravitch	"Diane Ravitch: Obama and No Child Left Behind," *Newsweek*, March 20, 2011.

CHAPTER 3

What Role Should School Choice Play in School Reform?

Chapter Preface

Prior to the establishment of public schools in the nineteenth century, the choices of whether or not children would attend school and what kind of education they would receive were up to parents and depended upon their choices and their finances. Today, the law demands that all children must receive schooling, but parents have a choice about whether that schooling is through public school, private school, or through homeschooling. In recent years, interest has grown in other ways for parents to have choice over the schools their children attend, such as by developing charter schools, enacting school vouchers, or allowing private school tax credits.

Charter schools provide an alternative to public schools. These schools receive public funding, and students can attend them for free. However, they are operated independently from traditional public schools; therefore, they are exempt from some state regulations, though not from student performance requirements. Thus, charter schools tend to be more experimental than traditional public schools and vary in their philosophies and performance outcomes. According to the National Alliance for Public Charter Schools, in the 2012–2013 school year there were more than six thousand charter schools, making up more than 6 percent of all publicly funded schools.

School vouchers give parents a voucher equivalent to the amount of money spent per child in public school for use at a private school of their choosing. Using public money for private school has always been controversial, primarily due to the concern that using vouchers for religious schools violates the establishment clause of the First Amendment that requires a separation of church and state. However, in 2002 the US Supreme Court held that an Ohio voucher program that used public funds to give parents vouchers to pay for education in religious and other private schools did not violate the US

Constitution. The court determined that as long as aid went directly to parents in the form of vouchers, there was no constitutional violation. According to the National Conference of State Legislatures (NCSL), as of August 2014, thirteen states and the District of Columbia offered student vouchers, many of which had low-income requirements.

Similar to school vouchers, tuition (or scholarship) tax credits are a way of offering school choice to parents by offsetting the cost. Tuition tax credits do this by allowing individuals and corporations to offset a portion of their owed state taxes by giving the amount to private, nonprofit, school-scholarship organizations that give scholarships to students to attend one of their approved private schools, which include religious schools. According to the NCSL, scholarship tax credit programs were used in fourteen states as of August 2014. Although the tuition tax credit programs do not directly give parents a voucher, by offering a reduction in taxes the program essentially amounts to a monetary transfer of government funds.

Whether through charter schools, school vouchers, or tuition tax credits, measures aimed at increasing school choice are not without controversy. There is widespread concern about the use of government funds for religious schooling, with many arguing that such a practice violates the First Amendment, even though the Supreme Court has said otherwise. Others claim that diverting resources from the existing public school system will worsen the quality of public education and that the programs primarily benefit families who already send their children to private school and have the resources to do so. However, supporters of school choice claim that since taxes are paid by all, these initiatives aimed at school choice simply support the rights of parents to choose how their children are educated. As the viewpoints in the following chapter illustrate, there are strong opinions for and against school choice measures.

Viewpoint 1

> *"Today, 18 voucher programs in 12 states and the District of Columbia help expand the educational options of millions of disadvantaged schoolchildren."*

School Vouchers Are a Good Way to Promote School Choice

Casey Given

In the following viewpoint, Casey Given argues that school voucher programs expand educational options and should be used to improve education for all students. Given claims that despite evidence to the contrary, three myths about school vouchers persist. He denies that school vouchers increase segregation, that they are not utilized effectively by low-income parents, and that school vouchers mask the real problem of poverty. Given is editor and policy commentator for Young Voices, a project that promotes millennials' policy opinions in the media.

As you read, consider the following questions:

1. What Nobel Prize–winning economist does Given credit with advancing the use of school vouchers in the United States?

Casey Given, "The Myths of School Vouchers, Then and Now," *Freeman*, January 27, 2014.

2. The author claims that in most school voucher programs, there are strict family income eligibility caps usually below what amount?
3. Over the past thirty years, the total cost of educating a child in the public school system has increased by what factor, according to Given?

Today [January 27, 2014] marks the first day of [National] School Choice Week, a national effort to promote educational options such as private school vouchers. Although the first voucher program in the United States was introduced in 1869, it wasn't until a century later that school choice started gaining mainstream traction, thanks to the efforts of Nobel Prize–winning economist Milton Friedman. In 1980, millions of Americans tuned in to watch Friedman make the case for choice while engaging in lively debate with opponents on his PBS television series *Free to Choose*.

A lot has changed in the 34 years since the program first aired. Today, 18 voucher programs in 12 states and the District of Columbia help expand the educational options of millions of disadvantaged schoolchildren. Despite this progress, many of the myths surrounding school choice raised by Friedman's intellectual opponents still persist, hindering the growth of vouchers to the universal scale that the economist originally imagined.

I will address three mentioned in *Free to Choose*: namely, that school vouchers lead to more segregated classrooms, that poor parents don't have sufficient information to make the best educational choices for their children, and that poverty is the primary cause of America's abysmal public school performance.

The Concern About Segregation

MYTH No. 1: School vouchers increase segregation. "I am concerned that voucher systems will lead towards havens for white flight, will lead towards a dual-school system, in the sense that you have one school system operating under one set of rules, the other school system, [the] public school system, operating under carefully articulated educational policy in any given state."—Thomas Shannon, president of the National [School Boards] Association

When *Free to Choose* was filmed, many education pundits worried then that the majority of applicants for Friedman's hypothetical vouchers would be parents from middle- and high-income backgrounds and that vouchers would act as an unnecessary subsidy for private schooling of the rich. Their fear made sense at the time, especially considering the historical legacy of "segregation academies" in the South, where a handful of local governments offered white parents vouchers for their children to escape integrated public schools after *Brown v. Board of Education.*

Fortunately, these fears have not come to fruition. In fact, almost every private voucher program in the country has strict family income eligibility caps for its participants—usually below 300 percent of the federal poverty line. Contrary to outdated fears of white flight, vouchers today make America's schools more diverse by empowering students from poor socioeconomic backgrounds to attend the same institutions as their middle- and high-income neighbors. A recent literature review by the Friedman Foundation for Educational Choice confirms this point, discovering that seven of eight studies examining vouchers' effects on diversity conclude that they lead to more integrated classrooms.

The [Barack] Obama administration must not have gotten the memo. In August, the Department of Justice [DOJ] sued Louisiana's state voucher program for allegedly violating federal desegregation orders, despite expert testimony from scholars like Boston University professor Christine Rossell demonstrating that the vouchers improved integration in several parishes.

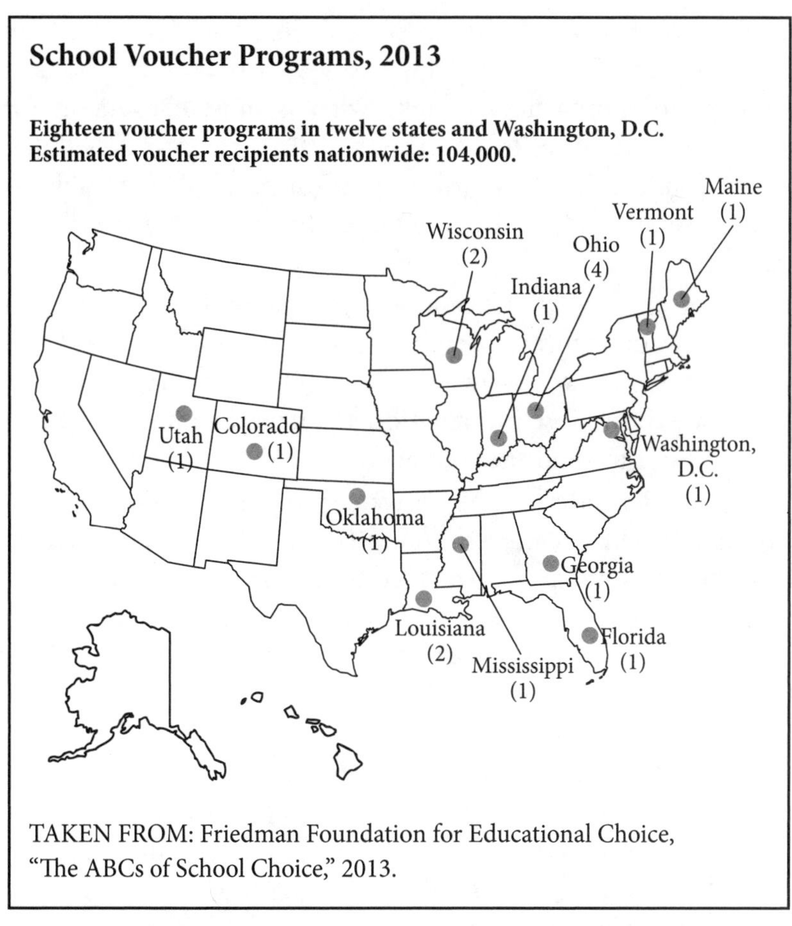

School Voucher Programs, 2013

Eighteen voucher programs in twelve states and Washington, D.C.
Estimated voucher recipients nationwide: 104,000.

TAKEN FROM: Friedman Foundation for Educational Choice, "The ABCs of School Choice," 2013.

While the DOJ eventually dropped its challenge after a federal judge ordered the agency to settle the matter out of court, the myth surrounding vouchers' supposedly segregating effects persists more than three decades after Shannon expressed it on *Free to Choose.*

The Concern About Low-Income Parents

MYTH No. 2: Poor parents don't have sufficient information to choose the best schools for their children. "And I think that the evidence is pretty clear that if you take middle class and wealthier families, they are gonna do a good deal of research. They may very well be able to invest some additional money of their own to take some inconvenience. And if you have an open system of this sort it may very well be that the poorest parents are gonna have to take what is most convenient for them, what is going to fit in with their own work schedules, what is not going to require additional sums of money."—Albert Shanker, president of the American Federation of Teachers

Choosing a school takes serious time and attention, with parents wading through endless statistics and paperwork. As such, contemporary voucher critics still worry that poor parents have imperfect information to make a sound choice of what school to send their child to.

Kern Alexander of the University of Illinois, for example, writes in the *Journal of Education Finance* that vouchers falsely assume "parents know what constitutes quality education." Since only educators are truly learned about education, so goes this line of reasoning, the public school system is in a better position to ensure a child receives a quality education than his or her parents are.

This view is quite simply unsupported by evidence. To the contrary, one survey on Georgia's voucher program commissioned by the Friedman Foundation discovered that "parents who are considered to be disadvantaged took about as many affirmative steps to gain the necessary private school information as parents having higher incomes." Both groups took an average of five steps to investigate school quality, most popularly touring the school and asking friends and family about its quality. Contrary to the patronizing myth, low-income parents are profoundly aware of the abysmal state of their children's schools and are thus motivated to escape a mediocre public school system just as much as their middle- and high-income neighbors.

The Concern About Poverty

MYTH No. 3: Poverty, not teacher quality, is the root of America's educational woes. "With all respect, Professor, the problems that you see in the urban schools of this country are not problems of the schools, they are problems of poverty. And they are problems of what do you do when, for demographic and sociological and economic reasons, in a country like ours, you begin to concentrate those people who are poor in the inner and older parts of the cities of our country."—Gregory Anrig, commissioner of the Massachusetts Department of Education

While the first two myths mentioned manifest themselves in subtler forms now than they did when *Free to Choose* first aired, this last one has only been amplified through the years. Today, income inequality is the main mantra of voucher opponents, with pundit after pundit pointing to poverty, not teacher quality, as the underlying problem in America's public school system.

"America does not have a general education crisis; we have a poverty crisis," Michael A. Rebell and Jessica R. Wolff of Columbia University's Campaign for Educational Equity claim in a recent article for *Education Week*, pointing to the latest test results from the Programme for International Student [Assessment]. "U.S. schools with fewer than 25 percent of their students living in poverty rank first in the world among advanced industrial countries. But when you add in the scores of students from schools with high poverty rates, the United States sinks to the middle of the pack."

Poverty's effect on student achievement is as undeniable today as it was during Milton Friedman's day. Children who come to school tired and hungry from an impoverished household will not perform as well as their peers who have a good night's sleep and food in their stomachs. However, mediocre performance by public schools is not an inevitable result of poverty. Such a status-quo bias ignores the fact that for many children, voucher programs have been an effective escape out of the cycle of poverty.

Study after study has confirmed that voucher recipients in America's most impoverished cities graduate high school and enroll in college at a higher degree than do their public school peers who were not selected for the program. To provide a few examples: The University of Arkansas came to this conclusion for graduation rates in Milwaukee's Parental Choice Program, the Brookings Institution did so for college enrollment in New York City's [School] Choice Scholarships Program, and the U.S. Department of Education did so for graduation rates in Washington, D.C.'s Opportunity Scholarship Program.

A lot has changed in American education since *Free to Choose* first aired, with school choice more popular and present than ever before. Yet, while private vouchers grow, the public school system continues to stagnate. Over the past 30 years, the total cost of educating a child in America's public schools has doubled after adjusting for inflation, while educational achievement as seen on the National Assessment of Educational Progress has stagnated.

If reformers truly want to improve the dismal state of America's schools, they should ignore the myths that persist 34 years after *Free to Choose* first aired and instead realize Friedman's vision of quality education for all children.

Viewpoint 2

> "Charter schools are finally becoming genuinely frightening to the powers that be in traditional public education, and for good reason."

Winning the War on Charter Schools

Reihan Salam

In the following viewpoint, Reihan Salam argues that charter schools continue to expand in the United States. Salam contends that the main barrier to further growth is unwarranted opposition from teachers and school administrators. He claims that teachers' unions and certain politicians perpetuate the fear of charter schools, but Salam contends that evidence is mounting for the view that charter schools are not only good for students but also good for teachers. Salam is a media fellow with the R Street Institute and a contributing editor at National Review.

As you read, consider the following questions:

1. Salam draws an analogy between the relationship of charter schools to public schools and the relationship of Amazon.com to what?

Reihan Salam, "Winning the War on Charter Schools," *National Review Online*, February 18, 2014. www.nationalreview.com.

2. The author identifies the mayor of what city as a staunch opponent of charter schools?
3. What does Salam say the charter schools in New Orleans and Washington, DC, are demonstrating to teachers?

The public charter school movement is entering a new phase. To put it bluntly, charter schools are finally becoming genuinely frightening to the powers that be in traditional public education, and for good reason. Charter schools have always been frightening to traditional public schools for the simple reason that they are granted wide autonomy to develop new instructional models, and most of the people associated with traditional public schools are afraid of change, or rather afraid of change that doesn't involve increasing compensation levels. This is true of the people associated with most organizations, public or private, but public schools have long been shielded from the entry of new start-ups that leave them no choice but to start doing things in new ways. Brick-and-mortar retailers might resent Amazon.com for forcing them to experiment with new pricing models, or to have to learn how to deliver their products across vast distances quickly and inexpensively, but they often have a hard time strangling innovative business models in the crib—for one thing, incumbent businesses are often divided amongst themselves as to how to respond to new threats. In contrast, traditional public educators benefit from (a) enormous political influence, a product of the size of the public education workforce and the organization of large swathes of this workforce into effective labor unions, which are keen to protect the interests of their median members; and (b) the fact that "business as usual" has prevailed for so long makes it easy for people to assume that newness is bad. You don't generally have competing unions of public school teachers with dramatically different attitudes towards charters, despite the fact that you have individual public school teachers who might be sympathetic, or who might think that the competition for talent among charter schools might actually leave them better off than they are under the unionized status quo. But unions, like all democratic organizations should, represent the interests of their *median* members, and it is generally true that the teachers who think they'd be better off in a more diverse, competitive educational landscape represent a minority.

So unionized public school teachers have, from the start, fought to limit the expansion of public charters and, to the extent possible, their organizational autonomy. For example, if public charters are required to be subject to the collective bargaining agreements that prevail in a given district, you've kind of defeated the point of having a charter school, which is to allow school administrators and teachers to experiment with new ways of doing things. This is all old news. The new news, or the newish news, is that after years of fighting these battles, public charters have nevertheless kept growing. In 2010–2011, public charters represented 5 percent of all K–12 public schools in the United States and approximately 3.65 percent of total public school enrollment. The National Alliance for Public Charter Schools claims that public charters enrolled 2.3 million students in 2012–2013, a number that, if correct, would represent a 4.6 percent share of all public school students. I find the notion that public charter enrollment experienced such a big leap from one school year to the next a little implausible, so we'll take these numbers with a grain of salt. But keep in mind that public charter enrollment is much higher than the national average in many jurisdictions. New Orleans, in which 79 percent of public school students are enrolled in charters, is the most prominent example, followed by Detroit (51 percent), and Washington, D.C. (43 percent). We now have living, breathing examples of "charter school districts," in which the local school district has largely abandoned command and control, and is slowly evolving into a new role as a regulator and as a guarantor of quality across a network of autonomous schools.

It is worth emphasizing that while critics of traditional public education tend to fixate on unionized public school teachers as the bitterest foes of new ways of organizing schools, public school administrators are also a big part of the problem. They too are accustomed to old ways of doing things, and they worry that unleashing new instructional models might create new headaches—how do we assess performance? How do we comply with existing regulations? Even when (supposedly) rigid union contracts *don't* get in the way of changing established practices, administrators are often unwilling to even attempt to do so, assuming they're even aware that they can. This defensive, risk-averse mentality is hardly limited to teachers.

Charter schools are in the news in part because the new mayor of New York City, Bill de Blasio, doesn't seem to like them very much. De Blasio has garnered outsized attention because he is the mayor of America's media capital, and his often-strident rhetoric on inequality neatly aligns with the sensibilities of many of those who cover him. And de Blasio has decided that treating public charters as public schools (which they are, insofar as they are government-financed, tuition-free schools established by the government in cooperation with teachers, parents, and civil society groups) is no longer an acceptable approach. In the past, public charters in New York City were allowed to share space with traditional public schools, thus allowing public charters to avoid having to rent space on the open market. Commercial rents in New York City are quite high, and schools require a fair amount of space. De Blasio has called for reversing this policy and charging market rent to public charters that locate in public school facilities. What is left unstated is that the city government has wide discretion to determine whether or not space is available

Charter School Participation

From school year 1999–2000 to 2011–12, the percentage of all public schools that were public charter schools increased from 1.7 to 5.8 percent, and the total number of public charter schools increased from 1,500 to 5,700. In addition to increasing in number, charter schools have generally increased in enrollment size over time.

For instance, the percentages of charter schools with the largest enrollment sizes (500–900 students and 1,000 or more students) increased from 1999–2000 to 2011–12, and the percentage of charter schools with the smallest enrollment size (under 300 students) decreased from 77 to 56 percent.

From school year 1999–2000 to 2011–12, the number of students enrolled in public charter schools increased from 0.3 million to 2.1 million students. During this period, the percentage of public school students who attended charter schools increased from 0.7 to 4.2 percent. Between school years 2010–11 and 2011–12, the number of students enrolled in public charter schools increased from 1.8 million to 2.1 million.

US Department of Education,
"The Condition of Education 2014," May 2014.

for rent, and it is easy to imagine that the city will see to it that the supply of seats magically starts to shrink. Carmen Fariña, the city's new chancellor, has announced that she intends to review charter school expansion plans, including plans that are well under way. She has also called for diverting resources from public charters to new efforts to expand the traditional public school model into early education. Essentially, the city's Department of Education has shifted from a stance of benevolent neutrality towards public charters towards one of hostility. Charter schools in New York City enroll a far smaller share of students than in New Orleans or D.C., and it looks as though the de Blasio administration intends to keep it that way. It is true, however, that many New York City public schools are granted limited autonomy while operating within the traditional system, complete with union contracts.

We don't know exactly how the political dynamic in New York City will play out. Public charters are unpopular within the de Blasio administration, which is led by people with strong ties to organized labor (the mayor and his chief deputy were both paid by 1199SEIU, the most powerful labor union, and arguably one of the most powerful entities of any kind, in New York State), yet they are considerably more popular with the wider public. Moreover, Matt Yglesias recently observed that charter schools are at the heart of the most serious ideological divide among Democrats at the national level, which means that de Blasio doesn't enjoy the support of all members of his expansive left-of-center coalition on this issue.

Even if we see significant backsliding on charter schools in New York City, the success of the Recovery School District (RSD) experiment in New Orleans has attracted considerable attention across the country. Neerav Kingsland, the CEO [chief executive officer] of New Schools for New Orleans and a champion of the public charter movement, has argued that the RSD model can be replicated across the country. Its central features are as follows: (a) instead of seeing itself as the operator of all local government schools, the RSD serves as a *market creator* that breaks the local government monopoly by attracting new charter schools and charter school networks into a given market, and that makes it easier for talented people to become teachers even if they haven't come through the traditional pipeline (e.g., mid-career professionals); (b) RSD leaders serve as ambassadors and talent recruiters for all local schools, regardless of who is running them; and (c) the RSD serves as a bankruptcy steward which intervenes when schools fail, either to bring in a new team to fix them or to close them down while facilitating the expansion of more successful schools. (In *The Urban School System of the Future*, Andy Smarick offers an even more ambitious blueprint, in which urban school districts evolve into stewards for all publicly funded schools, including private schools that agree to operate within certain strictures.)

The real barrier to the future success of the charter school movement isn't hostile local politicians like Bill de Blasio, who if anything is concentrating the mind of his opponents. Rather, it is the fear among teachers that the shift to a more diverse educational landscape won't be in their best interest. But New Orleans and Washington, D.C., are demonstrating that public charters aren't terrible places to work—in many cases, they're better places to work than traditional public schools, and they give teachers who've grown frustrated with one instructional model the opportunity to embrace another one. Champions of charter schools have tended to emphasize the good they can do for children, and for good reason. As the debate around charter schools enters a new phase, they ought to consider emphasizing the good they can also do for teachers.

Viewpoint 3

> *"Abandoning public schools for a free market system eviscerates our basic obligation to support them."*

Charter Schools Are a Bad Idea

Diane Ravitch

In the following viewpoint, Diane Ravitch argues that the growth of charter schools is privatizing education and increasing social problems. Ravitch claims that the original purpose of charter schools has been abandoned, and the reality of charter schools is a system of unregulated schools that, at best, are just as good as public schools. Ravitch concludes that instead of privatizing education, public schools need to be strengthened. Ravitch is Research Professor of Education at New York University and author of Reign of Error: The Hoax of the Privatization Movement and the Danger to America's Public Schools.

As you read, consider the following questions:

1. What was the original purpose of charter schools, according to Ravitch?

Diane Ravitch, "The Charter School Mistake," *Los Angeles Times*, October 1, 2013.

2. What is the greatest danger of charter schools, according to the author?
3. With what five other public goods does Ravitch draw an analogy to support her view that schools are not a consumer good?

Los Angeles has more charter schools than any other school district in the nation, and it's a very bad idea.

The Original Purpose of Charter Schools

Billionaires like privately managed schools. Parents are lured with glittering promises of getting their kids a sure ticket to college. Politicians want to appear to be champions of "school reform" with charters.

But charters will not end the poverty at the root of low academic performance or transform our nation's schools into a high-performing system. The world's top-performing systems—Finland and Korea, for example—do not have charter schools. They have strong public school programs with well-prepared, experienced teachers and administrators. Charters and that other faux reform, vouchers, transform schooling into a consumer good, in which choice is the highest value.

The original purpose of charters, when they first opened in 1990 (and when I was a charter proponent), was to collaborate with public schools, not to compete with them or undermine them. They were supposed to recruit the weakest students, the dropouts, and identify methods to help public schools do a better job with those who had lost interest in schooling. This should be their goal now as well.

Instead, the charter industry is aggressive and entrepreneurial. Charters want high test scores, so many purposely enroll minimal numbers of English language learners and students with disabilities. Some push out students who threaten their test averages. Last year [2012], the federal [Government] Accountability Office issued a report chastising charters for avoiding students with disabilities, and the ACLU [American Civil Liberties Union] is suing charters in New Orleans for that reason.

The Reality of Charter Schools

Because they are loosely regulated, charter schools are often neither accountable nor transparent. In 2013, the founders of an L.A. charter with 1,200 students were convicted of misappropriating more than $200,000 in public funds. In Oakland, an audit at the highest-performing charter schools in the state found that $3.8 million may have been misused when the founder hired his other businesses to do work for his charters.

Charter schools are "public" when it is time to claim public funding, but they have claimed in federal court and before the National Labor Relations Board to be private corporations when their employees seek the protection of state labor laws.

In Los Altos, a group of wealthy people opened a boutique charter school for their own children. Parents are asked to donate $5,000 per child each year. Local public school parents consider the charter to be an elite private school, albeit one primarily funded with public dollars.

Of course there are honorable, well-run charter schools that provide an excellent education. This newspaper's [*Los Angeles Times*] editorial board cites independent research that shows students in L.A. charters do better than they would in L.A. [public] schools. But many other studies show that charters in general are no more successful at the task of educating children than public schools if they enroll the same kinds of students.

The Greatest Danger

As large as the gulf can be between charter cheerleading and charter reality, it doesn't represent the greatest danger of these schools. They have become the leading edge of a long-

The Impact of Charter Schools

In too many places, charters function more like deregulated "enterprise zones" than models of reform, providing subsidized spaces for a few at the expense of the many. They drain resources, staff, and energy for innovation away from other district schools. . . . This is especially a problem in big city public systems that urgently need renewal and resources but are increasingly being left behind. . . .

None of this is meant to deny the reform impulse that is a real part of the charter movement, and no one questions the desire of parents to find the best options they can for their children. But the original idea behind charter schools was to create "laboratories for innovation" that would nurture reform strategies to improve the public system as a whole. That hasn't happened.

Stan Karp, "How Charter Schools Are Undermining the Future of Public Education," AlterNet, November 14, 2013.

cherished ideological crusade by the far right to turn education into a consumer choice rather than a civic obligation.

Abandoning public schools for a free market system eviscerates our basic obligation to support them whether our own children are in public schools, private schools or religious schools, and even if we have no children at all.

The campaign to "reform" schools by turning public money over to private corporations is a great distraction from our system's real problems: Academic performance is low where poverty and racial segregation are high. Sadly, the U.S. leads other advanced nations of the world in the proportion of children living in poverty. And income inequality in our nation is larger than at any point in the last century.

The Way to Improve Education

We should do what works to strengthen our schools: Provide universal early childhood education (the U.S. ranks 24th among 45 nations, according to the *Economist*); make sure poor women get good prenatal care so their babies are healthy (we are 131st among 185 nations surveyed, according to the March of Dimes [Foundation] and the United Nations); reduce class size (to fewer than 20 students) in schools where students are struggling; insist that all schools have an excellent curriculum that includes the arts and daily physical education, as well as history, civics, science, mathematics and foreign languages; ensure that the schools attended by poor children have guidance counselors, libraries and librarians, social workers, psychologists, after-school programs and summer programs.

Schools should abandon the use of annual standardized tests; we are the only nation that spends billions testing every child every year. We need high standards for those who enter teaching, and we need to trust them as professionals and let them teach and write their own tests to determine what their students have learned and what extra help they need.

Our nation is heading in a perilous direction, toward privatization of education, which will increase social stratification and racial segregation. Our civic commitment to education for all is eroding. But like police protection, fire protection, public beaches, public parks and public roads, the public schools are a public responsibility, not a consumer good.

VIEWPOINT 4

> *"Despite the lack of proof that school-choice policies work, they are gaining popularity in communities nationwide."*

Why School Choice Fails

Natalie Hopkinson

In the following viewpoint, Natalie Hopkinson argues that the result of school reform intended to bring more school choice has been closed public schools for poor, black neighborhoods and more choices and better schools for wealthy, white neighborhoods. She contends that when failing schools close down they are in poor neighborhoods, and these schools are not replaced. Hopkinson says that the idea that parents of children of these schools have choice is false, as there is not enough room to accommodate all the students who want to go to the best schools in the wealthy neighborhoods. Hopkinson is a writer.

As you read, consider the following questions:

1. Hopkinson claims that in 1995, Washington, DC, implemented a reform policy allowing that if a school were deemed failing, one of what three things would occur?

Natalie Hopkinson, "Why School Choice Fails," *New York Times*, December 5, 2011, p. A27.

2. School reform is a great deal for whom, according to the author?
3. Hopkinson contends that communities considering school choice can choose between private schools and charter schools or what?

If you want to see the direction that education reform is taking the country, pay a visit to my leafy, majority-black neighborhood in Washington. While we have lived in the same house since our 11-year-old son was born, he's been assigned to three different elementary schools as one after the other has been shuttered. Now it's time for middle school, and there's been no neighborhood option available.

Meanwhile, across Rock Creek Park in a wealthy, majority-white community, there is a sparkling new neighborhood middle school, with rugby, fencing, an international baccalaureate curriculum and all the other amenities that make people pay top dollar to live there.

The Result of School Reform

Such inequities are the perverse result of a "reform" process intended to bring choice and accountability to the school system. Instead, it has destroyed community-based education for working-class families, even as it has funneled resources toward a few better-off, exclusive institutions.

My neighborhood's last freestanding middle school was closed in 2008, part of a round of closures by then mayor Adrian Fenty and his schools chancellor Michelle Rhee. The pride and gusto with which they dismantled those institutions was shameful, but I don't blame them. The closures were the inevitable outcome of policies hatched years before.

In 1995 the Republican-led Congress, ignoring the objections of local leadership, put in motion one of the country's strongest reform policies for Washington: If a school was deemed failing, students could transfer schools, opt to attend a charter school or receive a voucher to attend a private school.

The idea was to introduce competition; good schools would survive; bad ones would disappear. It effectively created a second education system, which now enrolls nearly half the city's public school students. The charters consistently perform worse than the traditional schools, yet they are rarely closed.

Meanwhile, failing neighborhood schools, depleted of students, were shut down. Invariably, schools that served the poorest families got the ax—partly because those were the schools where students struggled the most, and partly because the parents of those students had the least power.

A Boon for the Wealthy

Competition produces winners and losers; I get that. Indeed, the rhetoric of school choice can be seductive to angst-filled middle-class parents like myself. We crunch the data and believe that, with enough elbow grease, we can make the system work for us. Naturally, I've only considered high-performing schools for my children, some of them public, some charter, some parochial, all outside our neighborhood.

But I've come to realize that this brand of school reform is a great deal only if you live in a wealthy neighborhood. You buy a house, and access to a good school comes with it. Whether you choose to enroll there or not, the public investment in neighborhood schools only helps your property values.

For the rest of us, it's a cynical game. There aren't enough slots in the best neighborhood and charter schools. So even for those of us lucky ones with cars and school-data spreadsheets, our options are mediocre at best.

In the meantime, the neighborhood schools are dying. After Ms. Rhee closed our first neighborhood school, the students were assigned to an elementary school connected to a homeless shelter. Then that closed, and I watched the children get shuffled again.

A System with Many Losers

Earlier this year [2011], when we were searching for a middle school for my son—11 is a vulnerable age for anyone—our public options were even grimmer. I could have sent him to one of the newly consolidated kindergarten-to-eighth-grade campuses in my neighborhood, with low test scores and no algebra or foreign languages. We could enter a lottery for a spot in another charter or out-of-boundary middle school, competing against families all over the city.

The system recently floated a plan for yet another round of closings, with a proposal for new magnet middle school programs in my neighborhood, none of which would open in time for my son. These proposals, like much of reform in Washington, are aimed at some speculative future demographic, while doing nothing for the children already here. In the meantime, enrollment, and the best teachers, continue to go to the whitest, wealthiest communities.

The situation for Washington's working- and middle-class families may be bleak, but we are hardly alone. Despite the lack of proof that school-choice policies work, they are gaining popularity in communities nationwide. Like us, those places will face a stark decision: Do they want equitable investment in community education, or do they want to hand it over to private schools and charters? Let's stop pretending we can fairly do both. As long as we do, some will keep winning, but many of us will lose.

VIEWPOINT 5

> *"Only a free market in education is consistent with a rights-respecting society."*

The Entire Public School System Should Be Abolished

C. Bradley Thompson

In the following viewpoint, C. Bradley Thompson argues that government-run public schools should be shut down. Thompson contends that there should be a free market in education, allowing parents to have full control over decisions about their children's education. He claims that although there is opposition to the abolition of schools, it is morally required to eliminate the public school system. Thompson is a research professor at Clemson University and the executive director of the Clemson Institute for the Study of Capitalism.

As you read, consider the following questions:

1. The author draws an analogy between the argument in favor of the separation of what and his support of the separation of education and the state?
2. Thompson cites that abolishing the government school system is opposed by the education establishment, parents, and what movement?

C. Bradley Thompson, "Education in a Free Society," *Objective Standard*, vol. 8, Winter 2013–2014, pp. 32–36, 39–40, 47.

3. In support of his argument in favor of a free market in education, Thompson cites what three goods as examples where free markets function?

What is the proper relationship of school and state? In a free society, who is responsible for educating children? Toward answering these questions, consider James Madison's reasoning regarding the proper relationship of government and religion—reasoning that readily applies to the issue of education. In 1784, in response to Patrick Henry's call for a compulsory tax to support Christian (particularly Episcopalian) ministers, Madison penned his famous "Memorial and Remonstrance [Against Religious Assessments]," a stirring defense of religious freedom and the separation of church and state. The heart of his argument can be reduced to three principles: First, individuals have an inalienable right to practice their religion as they see fit; second, religion must not be directed by the state; and third, religion is corrupted by government interference or control. Few Americans today would disagree with Madison's reasoning.

The Separation of School and State

One virtue of Madison's response to Henry's bill is that its principles and logic extend beyond church-and-state relations. In fact, the principles and logic of his argument apply seamlessly to the relationship of education and state. If we substitute the word "education" for "religion" throughout Madison's text, we find a perfect parallel: First, parents have an inalienable right to educate their children according to their values; second, education must not be directed by the state; and third, education is corrupted by government interference or control. The parallel is stark, and the logic applies equally in both cases.

Just as Americans have a right to engage in whatever non-rights-violating religious practices they choose, so Americans have a right to engage in whatever educational practices they choose. And just as Americans would not grant government the authority to run their Sunday schools, so they should not grant government the authority to run their schools Monday through Friday.

Parents (and guardians) have a right to direct the education of their children. Parents' children are *their* children—not their neighbors' children or the community's children or the state's children. Consequently, parents have a right to educate their children in accordance with the parents' judgment and values. (Of course, if parents neglect or abuse their children, they can and should be prosecuted, and legitimate laws are on the books to this effect.) Further, parents, guardians, and citizens in general have a moral right to use their wealth as they judge best. Accordingly, they have a moral right and *should* have a legal right to patronize or not patronize a given school, to fund or not fund a given educational institution—and no one has a moral right or properly a legal right to *force* them to patronize or fund one of which they disapprove. These are relatively straightforward applications of the rights to life, liberty, property, and the pursuit of happiness—the rights on which America was founded.

But the educational system in America today systematically ignores and violates these rights. At its core, America's system of state-controlled education is *compulsory*. It involves force from top to bottom: The state forces children to attend its schools (or state-approved alternatives). It forces taxpayers—whether or not they use the schools—to pay for them. It dictates what is taught in the classroom through its mandatory curriculum. And it dictates how teachers are to teach the content, through its requirement and control of teacher certification.

The Government School System

Because a government school system violates rights in such a fundamentally crucial area of life—education—it constitutes, as Madison said of a religious establishment, "a dangerous abuse of power." Government should never be in the business of forcing or controlling the mind—and nowhere is this principle more important than with respect to the education of young minds. Unfortunately, many Americans today willingly accept this dangerous abuse of power.

Although most parents embrace the responsibility of feeding their children and wouldn't dream of letting the government dictate what will be put in their children's bodies, they relinquish the responsibility of educating their children and permit the government to dictate what will be put in their children's minds. Few Americans see that this is what they are doing, but this *is* what they are doing. Consider how this all begins.

One day, when a child turns five or six, his parents drive him to the local government school and say, "Good-bye." What the parents typically do not realize is that when they say good-bye to that child, they are literally and forever saying good-bye to *that* child—to that unique, irreplaceable child they have raised, nurtured, and loved since birth. When the child comes home in the days, weeks, and months ahead, he or she will have become a *different* person; his mind will have changed, his views of the world will have formed, his values will have developed. In time, he will have spent his formative years—seven hours per day, five days per week for thirteen years—at a government institution whose purpose is to indoctrinate him with state-approved ideas and values, regardless of whether his parents approve of those ideas and values. When it comes to state-run schools, as government school advocate Lester Frank Ward stated candidly in 1897, "the result desired by the state is a wholly different one from that desired by parents, guardians, and pupil." The goal of a compulsory, state-run educational system is to ensure that children conform to the desires of the state. Education *by* the state is education *for* the state.

Given such facts about government education, one conclusion is clear: America's system of government-run schools must be abolished. This is the only policy consistent with the rights of parents and guardians and with the proper purpose of government, which is to protect and not to violate rights.

The Resistance of Teachers and Parents

Abolishing the government school system will not be easy. The forces defending the status quo are powerful and entrenched. At present, three major groups support the current system, and many of their members will oppose all efforts toward establishing a free market in education.

The first of these, the education establishment—the teachers' unions, the so-called ed schools or teacher training institutions, and the government education bureaucracy—will, like Southern slaveholders, fight tooth and nail against the emancipation of America's children and their parents. Many people in the education establishment believe their jobs depend on maintaining the status quo—and in many ways they *do*. Many in the education establishment are incompetent and would not fare well if required to compete with the competent rather than rest on their laurels. And many in the establishment are simply not concerned with educating children and will do anything to keep their jobs, regardless of how bad the schools are or become.

But the education establishment is not the main obstacle to abolishing the government school system and adopting a free market in education. The greatest impediment to educational freedom is the American people themselves.

Most Americans have been convinced—in large part by the education establishment—that the "public" school system, despite its obvious failings, is the bedrock of our "democracy" and the source of our national prosperity. As regards the government schools, Americans have a kind of "Stockholm syndrome." They support the very schools in which they suffered profound abuse and on behalf of which their rights are routinely violated. Because I frequently cite the significance of this phenomenon, my former colleague, the historian Eric Daniels, has termed it the "Thompson Paradox": Most Americans recognize that the nation's education system is failing but nevertheless insist that *their* local government school is doing a great job of educating their children. Ironically, American parents express the highest degree of satisfaction with their local schools of any parents in the developed world, despite the fact that their children are among the worst performers on international tests. This dissonance is fueled by the education establishment, which spends millions of taxpayer dollars every year on propaganda to the effect that government schools are necessary, doing pretty well, and could be doing much better if only they had more money.

The School Choice Movement

The third obstacle to establishing a free market in education is the so-called school choice movement. Despite all of its rhetoric about freedom and choice, this movement does not promote freedom or choice in education; rather, it promotes the perpetuation of government schools and the expansion of government involvement in education.

The main way the school choice movement does this is by advocating vouchers, which are, in effect, food stamps for education. Voucher programs assume that children have a "right" to a tax-funded education and thus that taxpayers must be forced to support government schools and/or pay for vouchers. But if *real* rights are to be protected and if education is to be freed from government force, the premise that children have a "right" to a tax-funded education must be rejected, not embraced.

Further, vouchers undermine and corrupt private education by gradually turning private schools into government-

The Role of Parents in Government Schools

The role parents play in the system of government education is minimal to nonexistent. Parents today have virtually no control over the ideas or values taught at the school to which their children have been assigned by the government. Over the past 150 years, the government has acquired the authority to teach children values that were once the exclusive domain of mothers and fathers; it has done so on the supposition that it knows better than parents how to bring up their children and which values they should embrace.

Although in some school districts parents are given a token voice in school affairs, even this small role is granted by *permission* rather than by right. The view of government authorities and educators on this matter is that parents are an unenlightened, harmful influence on children during the formative years of their development.

C. Bradley Thompson,
"The New Abolitionism: Why Education Emancipation Is the Moral Imperative of Our Time,"
Objective Standard, *Winter 2012–2013.*

controlled schools. When government provides students with vouchers, government obviously has a say in where and how that money is to be used.

Finally, the purpose of voucher programs is to *reform* the existing system of government-controlled education by injecting some degree of choice and competition into it. The goal is to make a corrupt system more efficient and effective in order to save and perpetuate it. To the extent that vouchers marginally or temporarily improve education, they undermine efforts to do what morally must be done. They undermine efforts to *end* government involvement in education—and they extend the coercive reach of government into private schools.

If we care about protecting individual rights and enabling all American children—rich, poor, and in between—to receive a quality education, we must abolish government schools and establish a genuinely free market in education. . . .

A Free Market in Education

As the government school system is dismantled, more and more opportunities will arise for entrepreneurs and educators to pursue free market alternatives. And once the government school system is completely abolished, a fully free market will enable educational alternatives and opportunities we can only imagine.

Of course, we cannot specify in detail what a fully free market in education will look like, just as we cannot know what our computers or phones will be like in five years, never mind twenty or thirty years. What we can know is that, given the law of supply and demand and given the enormous value that parents place on education, education entrepreneurs—when left free—will innovate and compete such that educational alternatives and opportunities will expand, and costs of education will (generally) decrease.

To the extent that businessmen and educators are free to act on their judgment and to pursue profits, they can and will work to provide good education at affordable prices. That is the only way to make money in a free market. Likewise, to the extent that parents are free to act on their judgment, they will pursue the best educational opportunities they can find given the needs of their children and the money they can afford to pay; thus, parents will reward businessmen and entrepreneurs who provide good educational opportunities at affordable prices. The result is a win-win-win-win system in which businessmen, educators, parents, and students all profit and prosper.

When school leaders and teachers know they must compete for every child who might attend their school, and when they know that parents are always on the lookout for a better and less expensive product, they are more likely to deliver the kinds of education that their customers want at affordable prices. Quality goes up and prices go down. This is how a free market works, and we can see it in every sector to the extent that it is free.

Consider the cell phone industry or the clothing industry or the Lasik surgery industry, or any other relatively free sector of the economy. What you will see is that when people are free to produce and trade in accordance with their judgment, opportunities and alternatives multiply, and prices make economic sense. That's the way it works for *all* goods and services in a market economy. And education is no exception.

Ending the Government School System

In a free market for education, new schools would be created to meet the demand, resulting in a cornucopia of educational diversity. New for-profit and nonprofit schools would open. Existing private schools would expand. Church-run schools would open or expand. University- and college-run schools would open or expand. Schools run by major corporations such as Apple and Boeing would open or expand. Big chain schools owned and run by tutoring companies such as Sylvan Learning, small neighborhood schools run by voluntary associations of parents, and online private schools owned and administered by education entrepreneurs would open or expand. And, of course, homeschooling would thrive. . . .

Only a free market in education is consistent with a rights-respecting society. The principle of individual rights requires the separation of school and state, the full freedom of educators to produce and parents to purchase education services in a competitive market where providers and customers strive continually for better ideas, better methods, and better results—at lower costs.

Just as our forefathers successfully fought to end slavery, and their forefathers successfully fought to separate church and state, let us carry on the fight to expand freedom in America by ending the tyranny that is the government school system.

Periodical and Internet Sources Bibliography

The following articles have been selected to supplement the diverse views presented in this chapter.

Jeff Bryant	"The Ugly Truth About Charter Schools: Padded Cells, Corruption, Lousy Instruction and Worse Results," AlterNet, January 10, 2014.
Lindsey Burke	"Why Market Forces Are Good for Education," *Atlantic*, February 3, 2012.
Jeb Bush	"We Need School Choice Now," *National Review Online*, January 27, 2014.
David French	"In Defense of School-Choice Tax Credits," *National Review Online*, April 5, 2011.
Jack Jennings	"School Vouchers: No Clear Advantage in Academic Achievement," *Huffington Post*, July 27, 2011.
Stan Karp	"How Charter Schools Are Undermining the Future of Public Education," AlterNet, November 14, 2013.
Matthew McKnight	"False Choice: How Private School Vouchers Might Harm Minority Students," *New Republic*, April 15, 2011.
Kristin Rawls	"The Ugly Truth About 'School Choice,'" AlterNet, January 24, 2012.
C. Bradley Thompson	"The New Abolitionism: Why Education Emancipation Is the Moral Imperative of Our Time," *Objective Standard*, vol. 7, no. 4, Winter 2012–2013.
Herbert J. Walberg	"Breaking the Public Monopoly on K–12," *Defining Ideas*, September 12, 2012.

Chapter 4

Should Curriculum Content in Schools Be Reformed?

Chapter Preface

In the United States, public school curriculum is set by each individual state, with varying degrees of control given to local school districts and teachers. There are two main areas where calls for curriculum reform are particularly vocal and contentious: those regarding academic rigor, particularly in science and math, and those involving changes to curriculum based on religious or personal beliefs.

The Organisation for Economic Co-operation and Development (OECD) Programme for International Student Assessment (PISA) measures student performance in math, science, and reading. In 2013 the OECD reported the results of the 2012 PISA by ranking results of sixty-five member countries. The United States did not stand out. In math, US students were below average, with twenty-nine countries having higher scores. In science and reading, US students were just about at the average, with twenty-two countries faring better in science and nineteen doing better in reading.

Former secretary of education William J. Bennett criticized US efforts in math and science education in 2012, calling for reform that brings more math and science into school classrooms and in earlier grades. Bennett claimed that ranking of US students compared to other students worldwide should signal concern: "If the United States wishes to remain the most competitive and innovative country in the world—never mind just another competitive and innovative country in the constellation of industrial nations—this cannot stand." Yet experts, including New York University education professor Diane Ravitch, claim there is no crisis: "Let others have the higher test scores. I prefer to bet on the creative, can-do spirit of the American people, on its character, persistence, ambition, hard work, and big dreams, none of which are ever measured or can be measured by standardized tests like PISA."

While there are those who are concerned about the rigor of the current school curriculum, others are more concerned about the level of control that parents have over the content of their children's education. This is particularly true where religious views conflict with classroom teaching. According to a Pew Research Center poll in 2013, 33 percent of Americans reject the idea of evolution. Nonetheless, the theory of evolution is a standard part of biology education nationwide.

In 2014 Republican legislator from Missouri Rick Brattin offered a bill that would allow parents to pull their children out of high school biology classes if they did not want them to be exposed to the concept of natural selection, one mechanism of evolution. The bill did not survive initial hearings, but it illustrated one of the controversies surrounding public school curriculum.

As the authors of the viewpoints in the following chapter illustrate, there are several ongoing debates concerning current public school curriculum and the various proposals for how it ought to change.

VIEWPOINT 1

> *"We need better math education . . . to ensure that democracy can continue to function in a world made ever more complicated by new technologies that rely on sophisticated mathematics."*

Math Has to Be at Least a Little Boring

Konstantin Kakaes

In the following viewpoint, Konstantin Kakaes argues that a recent newspaper editorial is mistaken in thinking that mathematics should be studied in a manner more focused on application than abstract problem solving. Kakaes claims that such a suggestion misunderstands the nature of mathematics and underestimates its power. Kakaes claims that mathematics is a crucial part of any education and must be studied for its own sake. Kakaes is a journalist.

As you read, consider the following questions:

1. Kakaes discusses an editorial piece that he claims fails to appreciate what fact about mathematics?

2. The author claims that any sane definition of "critical thinking" must include what?
3. Kakaes believes that math can be exciting on its own, without reference to what two fields of application?

This weekend [December 8, 2013], after American students failed to impress on the international PISA [Programme for International Student Assessment] exams, the *New York Times* editorial board ran a piece asking, "Who Says Math Has to Be Boring?" By "boring," the *Times* apparently means any math that is substantive in a traditional sense: "arithmetic, pre-algebra, algebra, geometry, trigonometry." So let me answer the question: Anyone with an understanding of what math actually is believes it must sometimes be boring.

A Misunderstanding About Math

The crisis in mathematics education is, as the *Times* says, severe. It extends all the way to the editorial board of the newspaper, whose members do not appear to understand what mathematics is, how it is used in the sciences, or why it is important. The *Times*' solution, "a more flexible curriculum," is euphemism for erosion of already-lax standards that would only make our present problems worse. What should replace boring old quadratic equations and logarithms (which aren't really all that scary)? The *Times* is vague, emphasizing only that standards shouldn't stand in the way of "nontraditional but effective ways to learn." The *Times* doesn't specify what these novel ways of learning might be, either, but it does lament that too few high school students take engineering classes. Here's the thing, though: That's because to do most engineering at a level other than play-acting, you need to already have basic high school math and science mastered. This is like reacting to a study that shows 2-year-olds don't crawl fast enough by insisting they start running wind sprints. Later, the piece holds up as exemplars schools that teach computer programming. But programming—worthy in its own right—is not mathematics, and cannot substitute for it.

The *Times*' misunderstanding comes from a failure to appreciate that mathematics—even at the basic level taught to elementary, middle, and high school students—is an intellectual discipline with content intrinsic to itself. This content is important and can be made exciting and accessible without reference to the "real world."

Let's take a simple example: 3+5=8. It is useful to know this sum without reference to 3 apples and 5 apples, or 3 cars and 5 cars, or 3 computers and 5 computers. It is an abstract fact, just as knowing that 8x9=72 is an abstract fact. Understanding these abstractions then lets us turn to a multitude of real-world applications. It is the knowledge that 3 of *anything* and 5 of *anything* adds up to 8. Thinking about apples may help a young child learn to add in the first place, but it isn't a substitute for subsequently developing the abstract skill of addition, which requires practice. The *Times*' dichotomy between "real-world problem solving" and "traditional drills" does not exist. As in learning foreign languages, repetitive drills enable students to master techniques—of which addition is the simplest example—which can then be used to solve problems in the real world, and to develop more mathematical sophistication, which can then be bolstered by using new mathematical concepts in the real world. This is true in arithmetic, and also in algebra, geometry, calculus.

The Importance of Mathematics Education

The *Times* editorial rests heavily on the authority of Anthony Carnevale, an anti-intellectual economist. In his *Times* interview, he refers derisively to curricula that "teach a lot of stuff that digs up old white guys from Greece." He entirely misses the power of mathematics, which is that it is universal. Pythagoras's theorem was true 2,500 years ago. It is true today. It is true for white guys, for guys who are not white, and for

The Editorial in Question

For all the reform campaigns over the years, most schools continue to teach math and science in an off-putting way that appeals only to the most fervent students. The mathematical sequence has changed little since the Sputnik era: arithmetic, pre-algebra, algebra, geometry, trigonometry and, for only 17 percent of students, calculus. . . .

The system is alienating and is leaving behind millions of other students, almost all of whom could benefit from real-world problem solving rather than traditional drills.

New York Times,
"Who Says Math Has to Be Boring?,"
December 8, 2013.

women. It is true in distant galaxies and will remain true forever. As such, it's worth teaching. Proving that it is true is exactly the stuff of critical thinking, which the *Times* repeatedly says is important.

They never specify what "critical thinking" is. Surely any sane definition includes an understanding of mathematical proof. Many important proofs—such as the fact that there are an infinite number of primes or that the square root of 2 is irrational—are eminently accessible to high school students (and to precocious younger students).

As many have pointed out, the *Times* loves to chase trends. But what is needed in mathematics education is not a new faux trend ("a fundamentally different approach") but rather renewed attention to teaching teachers the basics well, so that they can then pass them on to students, as Hung-Hsi Wu, an emeritus professor at the University of California, Berkeley, has long advocated.

The *Times*' most misguided belief may be the insistence that the reason we need better math education is to train a new STEM [science, technology, engineering, and math] workforce. The real reason we need better math education is to equip citizens to understand the world they live in. We need better math education—for all students—to ensure that democracy can continue to function in a world made ever more complicated by new technologies that rely on sophisticated mathematics. This is achievable only once we realize that math can be made exciting and vital on its own, and not by reference to computer programming or robotics. And that sometimes, it just takes hard work and discipline to reach mastery.

Viewpoint 2

> "*Unlike literature, history, politics and music, math has little relevance to everyday life.*"

How Much Math Do We Really Need?

G.V. Ramanathan

In the following viewpoint, G.V. Ramanathan argues that the government warning many years ago about the importance of improving mathematics education was mistaken. Ramanathan claims that math scores have not improved, despite the attempts at "marketing" math. He contends that most people do not need math in their daily lives, and he claims that the people who do need it are doing very well. Ramanathan is professor emeritus of mathematics, statistics, and computer science at the University of Illinois at Chicago.

As you read, consider the following questions:

1. Ramanathan draws an analogy between the marketing of math and the marketing of what three products?
2. The author claims that a 2008 review by the Department of Education found that math scores for teenagers have done what since the 1980s?

G.V. Ramanathan, "How Much Math Do We Really Need?," *Washington Post*, October 23, 2010.

3. Ramanathan says that the United States has produced how many Nobel laureates since the year that "A Nation at Risk" was published?

Twenty-seven years have passed since the publication of the report "A Nation at Risk" [in 1983], which warned of dire consequences if we did not reform our educational system. This report, not unlike the Sputnik scare of the 1950s, offered tremendous opportunities to universities and colleges to create and sell mathematics education programs.

Unfortunately, the marketing of math has become similar to the marketing of creams to whiten teeth, gels to grow hair and regimens to build a beautiful body.

The Marketing of Math

There are three steps to this kind of aggressive marketing. The first is to convince people that white teeth, a full head of hair and a sculpted physique are essential to a good life. The second is to embarrass those who do not possess them. The third is to make people think that, since a good life is their right, they must buy these products.

So it is with math education. A lot of effort and money has been spent to make mathematics seem essential to everybody's daily life. There are even calculus problems showing how to calculate the rate at which the fluid level in a martini glass will go down, assuming, of course, that one sips differentiably. Elementary math books have to be stuffed with such contrived applications; otherwise they won't be published.

You can see attempts at embarrassing the public in popular books written by mathematicians bemoaning the innumeracy of common folk and how it is supposed to be costing billions; books about how mathematicians have a more clever way of reading the newspaper than the masses; and studies purportedly showing how much dumber our kids are than those in Europe and Asia.

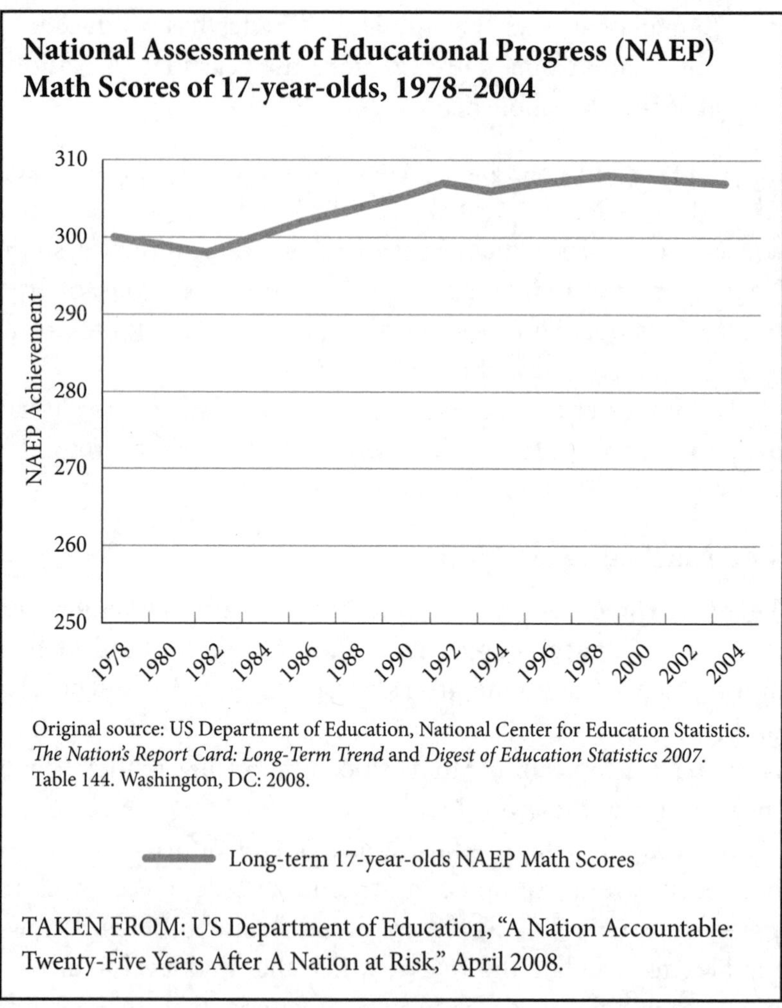

TAKEN FROM: US Department of Education, "A Nation Accountable: Twenty-Five Years After A Nation at Risk," April 2008.

As for the third, even people who used to proudly proclaim their mathematical innocence do not wish to abridge the rights of their children to a good life. They now participate in family math and send the kids to math camps, convinced that the path to good citizenship is through math.

Two Questions About Math Education

We need to ask two questions. First, how effective are these educational creams and gels? With generous government grants over the past 25 years, countless courses and conferences have been invented and books written on how to teach teachers to teach. But where is the evidence that these efforts have helped students? A 2008 review by the Education Department found that the nation is at "greater risk now" than it was in 1983, and the National Assessment of Educational Progress math scores for 17-year-olds have remained stagnant since the 1980s.

The second question is more fundamental: How much math do you really need in everyday life? Ask yourself that—and also the next 10 people you meet, say, your plumber, your lawyer, your grocer, your mechanic, your physician or even a math teacher.

Unlike literature, history, politics and music, math has little relevance to everyday life. That courses such as "Quantitative Reasoning" improve critical thinking is an unsubstantiated myth. All the mathematics one needs in real life can be learned in early years without much fuss. Most adults have no contact with math at work, nor do they curl up with an algebra book for relaxation.

The Need for Math

Those who do love math and science have been doing very well. Our graduate schools are the best in the world. This "nation at risk" has produced about 140 Nobel laureates since 1983 (about as many as before 1983).

As for the rest, there is no obligation to love math any more than grammar, composition, curfew or washing up after dinner. Why create a need to make it palatable to all and spend taxpayers' money on pointless endeavors without demonstrable results or accountability?

We survived the "New Math" of the 1960s. We will probably survive this math evangelism as well—thanks to the irrelevance of pedagogical innovation.

VIEWPOINT 3

> *"We find ourselves in danger of repeating the mistakes of the past in terms of trying to censor unpopular viewpoints in the classroom."*

Teachers Should Have the Freedom to Teach Critiques of Evolution

John W. Whitehead

In the following viewpoint, John W. Whitehead argues that recent attempts to silence critiques of evolution and the teaching of creationism in science classrooms violate academic freedom. Whitehead contends that a US Supreme Court decision in 1925 recognized that teachers should have academic freedom to teach evolution and creationism, but he laments the movement since 1968 toward teaching evolution exclusively. Whitehead, an attorney and president of the Rutherford Institute, is a proponent of academic freedom bills for teachers.

As you read, consider the following questions:

1. According to the author, the 1925 US Supreme Court trial of teacher John T. Scopes was concerning what Tennessee law?

2. According to Whitehead, why was teacher John Freshwater fired from his teaching job in Ohio?
3. According to Whitehead, do the new academic freedom bills passed in several states call for teaching intelligent design and creationism?

More than a century before Ohio science teacher John Freshwater found himself at the center of a battle over academic freedom in the classroom, namely, whether he has a right to urge his students to think critically about topics such as evolution, John T. Scopes faced a similar firing squad. In Scopes' case, however, he was prosecuted—or persecuted, as it were—for violating a Tennessee law, the Butler Act, prohibiting the teaching of evolution in state-funded schools.

Religion in Public Schools

While ostensibly about the debate over creationism versus evolution, Scopes' ensuing 1925 trial, immortalized in the award-winning play and film *Inherit the Wind*, presaged a shift in the way the nation relates to religion, particularly Judeo-Christian doctrines. This growing tension over the First Amendment's religion clauses, affirming freedom for the exercise of religion while prohibiting the government from establishing religion, continues to play out in the backdrop of the public schools. It is reflected in national debates over prayer in schools, the reference to God in the Pledge of Allegiance, and classroom discussions about the universe's origins.

The first U.S. trial to be broadcast on national radio, the Scopes Monkey Trial of 1925 [formally known as the *State of Tennessee v. John Thomas Scopes*], although initially contrived as a way to put Dayton, Tennessee, on the map, instead put the Judeo-Christian beliefs of a large portion of the nation on trial. Scopes, a high school science teacher, agreed to be the lead actor in a constitutional challenge to the state's prohibition on teaching evolution in its schools. Scopes threw down his proverbial gauntlet on April 24, 1925, when he led students in reading a section of a state-mandated textbook that explicitly described and endorsed the theory of evolution.

Charged with breaking the law, Scopes was put through an eight-day trial and a nine-minute jury deliberation before being found guilty and fined $100. On appeal to the Tennessee Supreme Court, Scopes' legal team argued that the ban on teaching evolution, rooted in a biblical worldview, violated the science teacher's right to free speech and the state's establishment clause. The Tennessee high court hinged its ruling in *State of Tennessee v. John Thomas Scopes* on the then dominant interpretation of the establishment clause, that the government could not establish a particular religion as the *state* religion. The Tennessee high court deemed the Butler Act to be constitutional because it did not establish a *single* religion as the state religion. (The Butler Act was a 1925 Tennessee law prohibiting public school teachers from denying the biblical account of humanity's origin.)

Following *Scopes*, the evolution/creationism debate underwent little change until the U.S. Supreme Court's 1968 ruling in *Epperson v. Arkansas*, which struck down an Arkansas statute similar to Tennessee's Butler Act. The case centered on a Little Rock, Arkansas, biology teacher who claimed the prohibition on teaching evolution was a violation of her First Amendment rights. Siding with the teacher, the court held that the U.S. Constitution prohibits a state from requiring teachers to conform to a particular religion. The court noted that "the state's undoubted right to prescribe the curriculum for its public schools does not carry with it the right to prohibit, on pain of criminal penalty, the teaching of a scientific theory or doctrine where that prohibition is based upon reasons that violate the First Amendment."

A Shift Away from Creationism

Epperson marked the beginning of a shift away from teaching creationism in the public school classroom toward teaching evolutionary theory. In the wake of the Supreme Court's landmark ruling, states began to grapple with whether evolution should be taught in *conjunction* with creationism, or if evolution should supplant creationism as the sole theory to be discussed in the classroom. While bans on teaching evolution were clearly unconstitutional, the looming question revolved around whether evolution and creationism could coexist as doctrines. Several states introduced legislation that would require "creation science" to be taught alongside "evolutionary science," and thus the academic freedom debate emerged.

Finally, in 1987, the United States Supreme Court effectively completed the national transition away from creationism and toward evolutionary theory in *Edwards v. Aguillard*, when it struck down a Louisiana act that required evolution and creationism to be taught together. Proponents of the act argued that the law protected the academic freedom of teachers. However, while the court ultimately held that the law violated the establishment clause, by no means did they slam the door shut on teaching creationism. In fact, the Supreme Court left open the possibility of teaching alternative theories about the origin of life as long as they are done with the intent to enhance the effectiveness of science instruction.

A quarter of a century later, evolution has supplanted creationism as the more focused area of instruction in the public school science classroom. Against such a backdrop, teacher John Freshwater's case reflects the ongoing tension between creationism and evolution, state-mandated curricula and academic freedom, and free speech versus political correctness, the latter having added a whole new layer of complications to what was once a primarily legal and moral discussion.

The Termination of a Teacher

In 2011 John Freshwater, a Christian with a 20-year teaching career at Mount Vernon Middle School in Ohio, was fired for encouraging his students to think critically about the school's science curriculum, particularly as it relates to evolution theories.

A graduate of Ohio University, Freshwater began teaching science at Mount Vernon Middle School in 1987 and proved himself an outstanding teacher, popular with the students and never once receiving a negative performance evaluation.

That all changed in 2008, when the Mount Vernon school board voted unanimously to begin termination proceedings against the veteran educator, citing concerns about his conduct and teaching materials, particularly as they related to the teaching of evolution. Earlier that year school, officials reportedly ordered Freshwater, who had served as the faculty appointed facilitator, monitor, and supervisor of the Fellowship of Christian Athletes student group for 16 of the 20 years that he taught at Mount Vernon, to remove "all religious items" from his classroom, including a Ten Commandments poster displayed on the door of his classroom, posters with Bible verses, and his personal Bible, which he kept on his desk. Freshwater agreed to remove all items except for his Bible.

Ironically, despite the school board's criticisms of Freshwater's methods, his students routinely outperformed other students, having earned the highest state standardized test scores of any eighth-grade science class in the district during the 2007–2008 academic school year. Freshwater was also the only science teacher at Mount Vernon Middle School to achieve a "passing" score on the Ohio achievement test, setting him ahead of his fellow educators.

The school board, however, wasted no time in initiating termination proceedings against Freshwater and suspending him without pay, prompting the veteran educator to request a public hearing. During the hearing process, which lasted almost two years, school officials were subjected to an outpouring of support for the beloved teacher, with students showing their support for Freshwater by organizing a rally in his honor and wearing T-shirts with crosses painted on them, as well as carrying Bibles to class.

A Battle in the Courts

On January 7, 2011, the hearing referee made a nonbinding recommendation that Freshwater be fired because "he persisted in his attempts to make eighth-grade science what he thought it should be—an examination of accepted scientific curriculum with the discerning eye of Christian doctrine." Despite the school board's own stated policy that, because religious traditions vary in their treatment of science, teachers should give unbiased instruction so that students may evaluate it "in accordance with their own religious tenets," the school board fired John Freshwater a week later, claiming that he improperly injected religion into the classroom by giving students "reason to doubt the accuracy and/or veracity of scientists, science textbooks and/or science in general."

With the help of the Rutherford Institute, Freshwater mounted a legal challenge in court, arguing that where a teacher's speech is in compliance with all board policies and directly relates to the prescribed curriculum, the school should not be permitted to terminate the teacher's employment as a means of censoring a particular academic viewpoint from the classroom. Waging an uphill and losing battle through the courts, Freshwater's case finally landed before the Ohio Supreme Court, which heard the case in February 2013.

Insisting that Freshwater has no claim to academic freedom that would allow him to teach evolution from a Christian perspective, school officials defended the firing. Reminding the court that academic freedom was once the bedrock of American education, Rutherford Institute attorneys argued that what we need today are more teachers and school administrators who understand that young people don't need to be indoctrinated.

Rather, they need to be taught how to think for themselves. "By firing John Freshwater for challenging his students to think outside the box" stated the institute, "school officials violated a core First Amendment freedom—the right to debate and express ideas contrary to established views."

Controversial Issues in the Classroom

Although Freshwater's teaching methods are at the heart of Mount Vernon's particular firestorm, teaching alternative theories in science classrooms in order to challenge students to think critically about what they are learning and enhance their education is not a particularly new approach. However, Freshwater's case does transform the age-old debate over creationism versus evolutionism into one over the extent to which teachers have a claim to academic freedom when teaching controversial issues.

While evolution may be at the heart of this particular academic freedom debate, a teacher's ability to present controversial views extends far beyond discussing the origins of life to explorations of world history, American politics, and other topics of import.

Such was the case of *Wilson v. Chancellor*. In 1976 a high school political science teacher, hoping to engage his students, invited four speakers espousing differing political viewpoints to his classroom, among these a Democrat, a Republican, a Communist, and a member of the John Birch Society. Despite the fact that the invitations were made with the express approval of the principal and local school board, members of the community objected, going so far as to circulate a petition demanding that the board's decision be reversed and threatening to vote out the school board members. In response, the board reversed its decision and banned all political speakers from the school.

When the case went to court, the district court ruled against the school board, finding fault with the board's rationale for reversing their decision, which hinged upon a fear of losing their seats, rather than any evidence that the speakers were incompetent or that the political viewpoints discussed

Americans' Views on Evolution and Creationism

Which of the following statements comes closest to your views on the origin and development of human beings—(human beings have developed over millions of years from less advanced forms of life, but God guided this process; human beings have developed over millions of years from less advanced forms of life, but God had no part in this process; (or) God created human beings pretty much in their present form at one time within the last 10,000 years or so)?

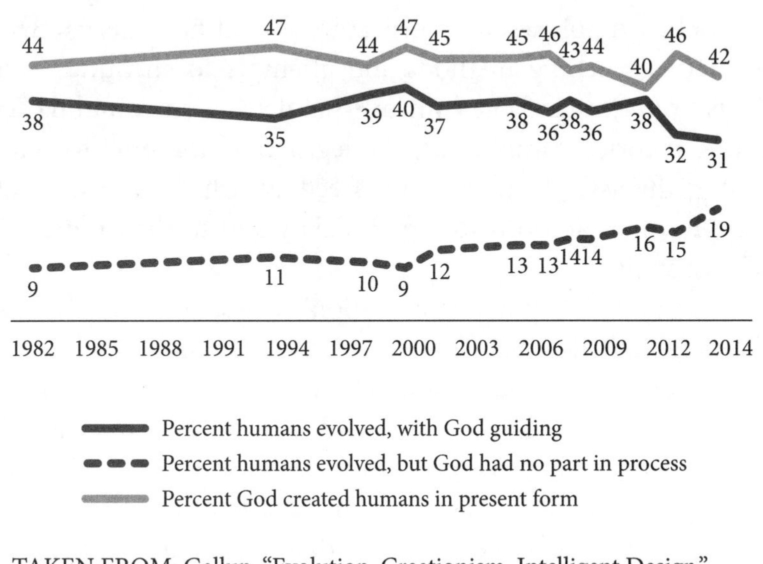

TAKEN FROM: Gallup, "Evolution, Creationism, Intelligent Design," 2014.

were inappropriate for a high school political science class. The end result: Teachers were allowed to invite political speakers to the classroom.

The Need for Academic Freedom

Recognizing that academic freedom is critical to providing a varied, in-depth, and quality education, especially in light of an increasingly politically correct climate that shows a certain disdain for all things religious, several states have adopted "academic freedom bills" in order to combat the intimidation, retaliation, and contempt teachers and students face when they attempt to discuss alternative theories and criticisms of evolution.

Unlike earlier, pre-*Aguillard* legislation, however, these bills do not call for teaching intelligent design and creationism as part of the school curriculum. Rather, academic freedom bills promote discussing evolution with a critical eye and acknowledging that evolution is, indeed, controversial. Further, these bills emphasize that, while teachers may be limited by certain school board policies, administrators should not interfere with the actual teaching methods and attempts to encourage students to understand the controversial debates surrounding scientific theories. Simply put, the legislation attempts to put a stop to the assault on academic freedom, which is seen as adverse to our traditions as a free society and to the progress of science itself.

Less than 100 years ago creationism was generally held as the *only* valid lesson plan for science classrooms, while the very notion of teaching evolution in our schools was controversial. Now the tables have turned, and we find ourselves in danger of repeating the mistakes of the past in terms of trying to censor unpopular viewpoints in the classroom.

Socrates, who once observed that "education is the kindling of a flame, not the filling of a vessel," would be justifiably horrified at America's present brand of rote education, so reliant on standardized tests and core curricula that there is little time to teach young people anything beyond the written curriculum, including how to think analytically and for themselves.

As the notable Greek philosopher concluded: "I cannot teach anybody anything. I can only make them think." Doubtless, John Freshwater would agree.

VIEWPOINT 4

> "Not only is it perfectly legal to teach about religion in unbiased and academically sound ways, but educators have a responsibility to do so."

Schools Should Teach About Religion

Mark Fowler and Marisa Fasciano

In the following viewpoint, Mark Fowler and Marisa Fasciano argue that schools need to teach students about religion. The authors claim that teaching about the differences in religious beliefs from around the world would help reduce hate crimes and ignorance while increasing religious literacy. Fowler and Fasciano claim that there is no constitutional barrier to teaching about religion as long as schools do not engage in practices that endorse a particular religion. Fowler is the managing director of programs and Fasciano is education program associate, both at the Tanenbaum Center for Interreligious Understanding.

As you read, consider the following questions:

1. According to the authors, what percentage of hate crimes were motivated by religious bias in 2012?

Mark Fowler and Marisa Fasciano, "Four Reasons Why You Should Teach About Religion in School," *Education Week*, April 5, 2014.

2. According to the authors, does the establishment clause of the First Amendment allow teachers to lead students in prayer?
3. According to the authors, does the free exercise clause of the First Amendment allow students to engage in private prayer at school?

For a variety of reasons, many educators are understandably reluctant to raise the topic of religion in the classroom. They may worry about offending a student, misrepresenting a tradition, or favoring one belief system over another. If you're unsure of the legal guidelines pertaining to religion in public schools, you might take the separation of church and state to its literal extreme and steer clear of the topic altogether.

Four Reasons to Teach About Religion

Addressing and overcoming this reluctance is essential to the creation of respectful learning environments that adequately prepare students for an increasingly diverse and connected world. Not only is it perfectly legal to teach *about* religion in unbiased and academically sound ways, but educators have a responsibility to do so. Here are four reasons why.

1. Religiously motivated hate crimes are on the rise.

According to the U.S. Department of Justice's "Hate Crime Victimization" report, the percentage of hate crimes that were motivated by religious bias was nearly three times higher in 2012 (28%) than in 2004 (10%). Many violent hate crime perpetrators are school age: In 2012, nearly one in five were under the age of 18. By encouraging students to understand and respect people of different religious beliefs, educators are combatting these disturbing statistics and contributing to a more peaceful world.

2. Our student body is more diverse.

In 1970, a little fewer than 5 percent of the U.S. population was foreign born. The majority of them were Christian

Europeans whose cultural and religious practices blended into the mainstream. By 2010, our foreign-born population has nearly tripled, and the proportion from Latin America (54%) and Asia (28%) greatly surpassed the proportion from Europe (13%).

To ensure that students of less familiar cultures and religious traditions feel included and safe in their learning communities, teachers need to provide opportunities for all students to share unique aspects of their identities. As their classmates become more educated about these differences, the likelihood of exclusivity and bullying diminishes.

3. Religious literacy is key to a well-rounded education.

If students are to function as globally competent citizens, they need to understand religion's profound impact on history, politics, society, and culture. They should know basic religious facts and principles and recognize the diversity that exists *within* each belief system across time and place. Familiarity with central religious texts is also important, and it's legal to study these texts in public schools, as long as the purpose is educational and not personal or devotional. For example, the Bible can be studied as a piece of literature that has influenced many classic works.

4. Students have a First Amendment right to religious expression in school.

The U.S. Constitution contains two clauses, known as the religion clauses, which inform the relationship between religion and public schools.

The establishment clause: "Congress shall make no law respecting an establishment of religion, . . ."

The free exercise clause: ". . . or prohibiting the free exercise thereof."

As government employees, public school teachers and administrators are subject to the establishment clause and thus

Americans' Results from a Religious Knowledge Survey

The survey results are clear: People with higher levels of education tend to be more knowledgeable about religion. College graduates get an average of 20.6 out of 32 religious knowledge questions right. Within this group, people who have a postgraduate degree (such as a master's degree, doctorate, medical degree or law degree) do even better, averaging 22.2 out of 32 questions correct, with 30% falling in the top 10% of all respondents (answering 26 or more questions correctly). Those with bachelor's degrees get roughly 20 questions right on average.

Scores are significantly lower among respondents with less education. Among people who have some college experience (but no degree), the average number of correct answers is 17.5. Those whose formal education ended with a high school diploma get 13.7 questions right on average. At the low end of the education spectrum, people who did not complete high school give an average of 10.7 correct answers on religious knowledge questions, roughly half as many as those with postgraduate degrees.

Pew Research Center,
"Factors Linked with Religious Knowledge,"
September 28, 2010.

required to be neutral about religion while carrying out their duties. The establishment clause prevents public school staff from

- mandating or organizing prayer;
- praying in the presence of students;

- indoctrinating students in a particular religious belief;
- religiously observing holidays;
- erecting religious symbols on school property;
- distributing religious literature for persuasive purposes; or
- displaying a preference for religion over non-religion, or vice versa.

The free exercise clause, on the other hand, affirms that certain religious activity in public schools is protected. As long as students do not coerce or otherwise infringe on the rights and learning of their schoolmates, they can

- engage in private prayer during the school day;
- express their religious beliefs in homework, artwork, and other written and oral assignments that meet educational goals; and
- obtain excusals from specific classroom discussions or activities for religious reasons.

Even though these guidelines may seem clear in the abstract, applying them to real-life situations often leaves room for interpretation and comes down to a judgment call. Educators can find it challenging to balance the requirements of the establishment clause, and the desire to protect students from unwelcome religious persuasion, with the right to free expression. To better prepare for this challenge, educators need to create conditions in their schools that allow for regular and sensitive communication about religious differences. That way, if religious tensions arise, they can be resolved more skillfully and effectively.

Dr. James Banks, a renowned expert in social studies and multicultural education, states, "The world's greatest problems do not result from people being unable to read and write.

They result from people in the world—from different cultures, races, religions, and nations—being unable to get along and to work together to solve the world's intractable problems." By replacing anxiety about religion with a thoughtful strategy for promoting students' religious literacy, educators are taking a step towards a better world.

Viewpoint 5

> *"'Teaching about religions' is one of those sparkling educational ideas that looks wonderful on paper, but, in fact, leads to dangerous madness."*

Allowing Schools to Teach About Religion Is Dangerous

Kevin Ryan

In the following viewpoint, Kevin Ryan argues that the idea to teach about religion in schools sounds good in theory but is a terrible idea in practice. Ryan contends that religion is not a proper field of study and, as such, there are no easy answers to questions about how to teach it or how to train teachers on the subject. He worries that students are not able to grasp knowledge about religion, especially if the topic is taught in a secular school that completely ignores issues of ethics and the meaning behind the religion's tenets. Ryan founded the Center for Character and Social Responsibility at Boston University, where he is professor emeritus.

As you read, consider the following questions:

1. According to the author, what was the US Supreme Court's ruling in *Abington School District v. Schempp*?

Kevin Ryan, "Should Schools Teach About Religions? It's an Idea That Looks Good on Paper but Can in Fact Lead to Dangerous Madness," Mercatornet, September 29, 2013. www.mercatornet.com.

2. The author worries that what religious traditions are already not treated with respect in schools?
3. Ultimately, the debate about teaching religion causes the author to raise what larger question?

Fifty years ago this past summer [2013], the United States Supreme Court issued a ruling that is still inflaming tempers and broiling controversies. The court banned prayer and advocacy teaching of religion in public schools. The case was the *Abington School District v. Schempp*, brought by young Mr. Schempp who believed that his constitutional rights were being violated by a Pennsylvania law allowing prayer and the reading of the King James Bible in his school. Schempp won and all hell broke loose. Ever since, civil libertarian groups and fundamentalists of many stripes had been warring. However, the war is dwindling down now to the occasional hand grenade in the form of an op-ed piece.

The Proposal to Teach About Religion

Such a grenade appeared earlier this summer in the *Wall Street Journal*, America's most widely read newspaper. It was a very cheery little column entitled "God Is Still in the Classroom" and the author made two points.

The first is that the Supreme Court's ruling was correct. It overwhelming ruled [8 to 1] that as government-sponsored schools, they must observe strict neutrality in matters of religion. As a former public school teacher and parent, I fully support such a decision. Paying tax money to a school that is promoting to my children a different religion from mine is cause for "going to the mattresses."

The article's second point was a celebration of the fact that public school can and should teach *about religion* and that, indeed, there is a good deal of teaching about religion going on in public schools today. Specifically, the author, a professor of religion, asserted that public schools can and should teach comparative and world religions and the Holy Bible as literature and history.

A week later in a letter to the editor, a teacher cast a shadow on this optimism: "I found that Judeo-Christian traditions are treated with suspicion and outright hostility, while pagan and animistic belief systems are considered academically interesting, but aren't taken seriously as religious faiths." This echoes reports I have heard over and over that Christianity, and particularly the Catholic Church, is a regular target for arched eyebrows, snide comments and direct ridicule in American public schools.

The Problems with Teaching About Religions

"Teaching about religions" is one of those sparkling educational ideas that looks wonderful on paper, but, in fact, leads to dangerous madness. Take for instance the comparative or world religion courses. How many high school teachers are equipped to convey properly to adolescents the theological and historical underpinnings of the great faiths? When they get around to Catholicism, how will they explain the Eucharist, the central reality of the Catholic faith? When they get into the history of the church will they address the centuries of good works done around the world by nuns and priests and committed laymen? Or will they drag out the inquisition and the history of the papacy? How about a "fair and balanced" treatment of the fourteen-century-old rift between Sunni and Shiite Muslims? And the three major branches of Judaism?

And where are these teachers to be trained? Have they taken one or two college courses in religion at the state university? At Georgetown University? Or are they self-trained? Can they be objective and fair, not favoring their "home team?"

And what about the students, the majority of whom have only the slimmest grasp of their own faith? Are they ready to "compare and contrast" Christianity and Zoroastrianism? Ready to probe the tenets of atheism and deism? In the current parlance, what is their "take away" from these courses? "All religions are equally weird." Or, "as a result of this course I believe the Mormons have the best take on the afterlife and the agnostics have the best sexual ethics." Or that favorite of the village atheist, "religion is just something men developed to explain the unexplainable and to keep us from being afraid of the dark."

Religion isn't, like sociology or literature or even theology, a field of study. Nor in the secular environment of a public school should it be. Religion is a personal belief system that directs the religious individual's answer to life's big questions, ultimate questions, such as: What is the meaning of my existence? What is a worthy way for me to spend my life? And how should I treat those around me? These are some of the fundamental human questions serious religions attempt to answer. These are questions for which our children need answers.

The Problem with Secular Education

Religion is and historically has been a central concern of U.S. citizens. Our Constitution rests on a religious view that all men are *created equal*. Our laws rest on the assumption of the *sanctity of the person* and that we have been *endowed* with certain rights. However, our educational system which increasingly dominates the lives of our children provides no understanding of these ideas. Mouth them, yes. Explore them? Teach them? No. They are just slogans in a world of competing slogans. "Be all you can be." "Do it!" "Things go better with Coke."

All children, intellectually gifted and not, seek to understand their world and what they should do to survive and prosper. Psychologists label us as "meaning seekers." When a child asks himself or herself "Who am I? What am I?" our public schools answer, "You are a future citizen, a future worker and taxpayer." When students ask themselves in the secret of their hearts, "Why be good? Why share? Why follow all these rules?," there is a pause and the schools answer, "Why it is in your *self-interest* to share and play by the rules."

The self-interest reasons, in general, work well with the children of the rich and those whose natural talents and abilities open up a vision of a prosperous future. Increasingly, however, those with lesser futures, those of limited talents and prospects, are realizing that their self-interest lies along less approved paths. They see the answer to getting what they want as rejecting the constraints of authority, as using others for their own gain or mere satisfaction, and as simply taking whatever brings them pleasure or eases their pain. These are the overriding messages behind the public schools' English literature and social studies courses, behind the world of athletics and extracurricular activities.

We have succeeded in building a huge and expensive mechanism to educate and, yes, socialize our children, but one that by law has excluded the core questions of human existence. In the U.S. today, the parents of 90 percent of our children have little choice but to send them to schools that provide a soul-shrinking view of what it is to be a human being. As a result, we have put their future and the future of the nation in the hands of a coming generation which has been nurtured by a pleasure-drugged culture. We have added to that a secular educational system that nourishes their hunger to understand how they should live their lives with empty bromides such as "Commit random acts of kindness." When that voice in their heads asks, "Why?," there is silence.

While it is legally and morally correct to keep the teaching of religion out of tax-supported, state-run schools, our current arrangement begs a larger question: Why should the state be in charge of what goes into the heads of children? Providing the resources for schooling from taxes is one thing. Deciding what is and is not to be learned is wrong . . . and, again, dangerous.

Periodical and Internet Sources Bibliography

The following articles have been selected to supplement the diverse views presented in this chapter.

Daniel H. Bowen and Collin Hitt	"High-School Sports Aren't Killing Academics," *Atlantic*, October 2, 2013.
David E. Drew	"The Five Misconceptions About Teaching Math and Science," *Slate*, June 19, 2012.
Jessica Lahey	"Confusing Math Homework? Don't Blame the Common Core," *Atlantic*, April 3, 2014.
Joseph Laycock	"We Must Teach About Religion in High Schools," *Religion & Politics*, January 7, 2014.
Tom Loveless	"The Curriculum Wars," *Defining Ideas*, March 20, 2014.
Peggy Noonan	"The Trouble with Common Core," *Wall Street Journal*, May 7, 2014.
Kathleen Porter-Magee and Sol Stern	"The Truth About Common Core," *National Review Online*, April 3, 2013.
Amanda Ripley	"The Case Against High-School Sports," *Atlantic*, September 18, 2013.
Phyllis Schlafly	"National Takeover of School Curriculum," *Townhall*, February 25, 2014.
Kurt Williamsen	"The Ruling Religion in Schools," *New American*, January 9, 2012.

For Further Discussion

Chapter 1

1. After reading the viewpoints by the Council of Chief State School Officers and Marion Brady, do you think the Common Core State Standards Initiative is beneficial or detrimental to education? Explain your reasoning, citing text from the viewpoints to support your answer.
2. Richard A. Epstein and Amy B. Dean take opposing viewpoints on the value of teachers' unions. How do you think Epstein would respond to Dean's suggestion that teachers' unions can be a positive force for education by becoming more engaged in the community? Explain your reasoning.

Chapter 2

1. Mary Elizabeth Williams, Herbert J. Walberg, and Virginia Myers all have different opinions on the effectiveness of standardized testing. Explain how you think Walberg would respond to the viewpoint of either Williams or Myers. Pick a specific argument of one of the two and identify specific text in Walberg's viewpoint to back up your response.
2. Amanda Ripley argues that students should have a role to play in teacher assessment. After reading the viewpoint, do you agree or disagree with Ripley's argument? Explain your reasoning.

Chapter 3

1. Reihan Salam argues that charter schools are not only good for students but also good for teachers. Diane Ravitch, on the other hand, says that charter schools are privatizing education and increasing social problems. With which author do you agree more, and why?

2. C. Bradley Thompson believes that school and state should be separate and that a free market in education should be established. Do you think a free market educational system would work in the United States? Explain your reasoning.

Chapter 4

1. Konstantin Kakaes says that students "need better math education . . . to function in a world made ever more complicated by new technologies that rely on sophisticated mathematics." How do you think G.V. Ramanathan would respond to this claim? Cite specific text from Ramanathan's viewpoint to support your answer.
2. Mark Fowler and Marisa Fasciano advocate teaching about religion in public schools, but Kevin Ryan raises concerns about the actual implementation of such a plan. How do you think Fowler and Fasciano would respond to Ryan's concerns? Explain.

Organizations to Contact

The editors have compiled the following list of organizations concerned with the issues debated in this book. The descriptions are derived from materials provided by the organizations. All have publications or information available for interested readers. The list was compiled on the date of publication of the present volume; the information provided here may change. Be aware that many organizations take several weeks or longer to respond to inquiries, so allow as much time as possible.

American Federation of Teachers (AFT)
555 New Jersey Avenue NW, Washington, DC 20001
(202) 879-4400
website: www.aft.org

The American Federation of Teachers (AFT) is a labor union that represents teachers, school-related personnel, higher education faculty and staff, government employees, and health care professionals. The AFT aims to advance fairness; democracy; economic opportunity; and high-quality public education, health care, and public services through community engagement, organizing, collective bargaining, and political activism. The AFT publishes numerous periodicals, including *American Teacher* and *American Educator.*

Americans United for Separation of Church and State (AU)
1301 K Street NW, Suite 850, Washington, DC 20005
(202) 466-3234 • fax: (202) 466-2587
e-mail: americansunited@au.org
website: www.au.org

Americans United for Separation of Church and State (AU) is a nonprofit educational organization dedicated to preserving the constitutional principle of church-state separation. AU works to defend religious liberty in Congress and state legislatures, aiming to ensure new legislation and policy protects church-state separation. AU publishes several books and pamphlets, including "Religion in the Public Schools: A Road Map for Avoiding Lawsuits and Respecting Parents' Legal Rights."

Brookings Institution
1775 Massachusetts Avenue NW, Washington, DC 20036
(202) 797-6000
e-mail: communications@brookings.edu
website: www.brookings.edu

The Brookings Institution is a nonprofit public policy organization that conducts independent research. Brookings uses its research to provide recommendations that advance the goals of strengthening American democracy, fostering social welfare and security, and securing a cooperative international system. The institution publishes a variety of research through the Brown Center on Education Policy, including the annual "Brown Center Report on American Education."

Carnegie Foundation for the Advancement of Teaching
51 Vista Lane, Stanford, CA 94305
(650) 566-5100 • fax: (650) 326-0278
website: www.carnegiefoundation.org

The Carnegie Foundation for the Advancement of Teaching is an independent policy and research center that aims to improve teaching and learning. The foundation aims to integrate the discipline of improvement science into education. It publishes numerous books and pamphlets, such as "Organizing Schools for Improvement: Lessons from Chicago."

Center for American Progress (CAP)
1333 H Street NW, 10th Floor, Washington, DC 20005
(202) 682-1611
website: www.americanprogress.org

The Center for American Progress (CAP) is a nonpartisan educational institute dedicated to improving the lives of Americans through progressive ideas and action. CAP develops new policy ideas, critiques the policy that stems from conservative values, challenges the media to cover the issues that truly matter, and attempts to shape the national debate. CAP publishes numerous research papers, including "Looking at the Best Teachers and Who They Teach."

Center for Education Reform (CER)
1901 L Street NW, Suite 705, Washington, DC 20036
(800) 521-2118
website: www.edreform.com

The Center for Education Reform (CER) aims to improve the accuracy and quality of discourse and decisions about education reform, leading to fundamental policy changes. CER campaigns for policies that create more educational choice, including the establishment of charter schools. The CER website offers numerous articles on the issues of charter schools, online learning, teacher quality, and testing, including "America's Attitudes Towards Education Reform: Public Support for Accountability in Schools."

Center for Public Education
1680 Duke Street, Alexandria, VA 22314
(703) 838-6722 • fax: (703) 548-5613
e-mail: centerforpubliced@nsba.org
website: www.centerforpubliceducation.org

The Center for Public Education is a resource center set up by the National School Boards Association. The center works to provide information about public education, leading to greater understanding of US schools, more community-wide involvement, and better decision making by school leaders on behalf of all students in their classrooms. Among the many publications available at the center's website is "Time in School: How Does the US Compare?"

Center for Science and Culture (CSC)
Discovery Institute, 208 Columbia Street, Seattle, WA 98104
(206) 292-0401

e-mail: cscinfo@discovery.org
website: www.discovery.org/csc

The Center for Science and Culture (CSC) is a Discovery Institute program that supports research by scientists and other scholars challenging various aspects of neo-Darwinian theory and developing the theory of intelligent design. CSC also encourages schools to focus more on weaknesses of the theory of evolution in science education. CSC has numerous papers, policy positions, and videos available on its website, including "Teaching About Evolution in the Public Schools: A Short Summary of the Law."

Center on Education Policy (CEP)
2129 G Street NW, 1st Floor, Washington, DC 20052
(202) 994-9050 • fax: (202) 994-8859
e-mail: cep-dc@cep-dc.org
website: www.cep-dc.org

The Center on Education Policy (CEP) is a national, independent advocate for public education and more effective public schools. The organization works on national, state, and local levels to inform the government and the public about the importance of the public education system through publications, meetings, and presentations. Reports on issues regarding all aspects of the education system, such as federal education programs, testing, vouchers, and ways to improve public schools, can be found on the CEP website.

Education Commission of the States (ECS)
700 Broadway, #810, Denver, CO 80203-3442
(303) 299-3600 • fax: (303) 296-8332
e-mail: ecs@ecs.org
website: www.ecs.org

The Education Commission of the States (ECS) is an interstate compact created in 1965 to improve public education by facilitating the exchange of information, ideas, and experiences among state policy makers and education leaders. As a nonprofit, nonpartisan organization involving key leaders from all levels of the education system, ECS creates unique opportunities to build partnerships, share information, and promote the development of policy based on available research and strategies. ECS provides policy research and analysis on current educational issues; sponsors state, regional, and national policy conferences; and publishes the bimonthly journal *The Progress of Education Reform*.

Friedman Foundation for Educational Choice
One American Square, Suite 2420, Indianapolis, IN 46282
(317) 681-0745 • fax: (317) 681-0945
website: www.edchoice.org

The Friedman Foundation for Educational Choice aims to promote universal school choice as the most effective and equitable way to improve the quality of K–12 education in America. The foundation was founded upon the ideals and theories of Nobel laureate Milton Friedman and economist Rose D. Friedman who believed that when schools are forced to compete to keep the children they educate, all parties win. The Friedman Foundation publishes studies and reports, including "More than Scores: An Analysis of Why and How Parents Choose Private Schools."

Heritage Foundation
214 Massachusetts Avenue NE, Washington, DC 20002-4999
(202) 546-4400
e-mail: info@heritage.org
website: www.heritage.org

The Heritage Foundation is a research and educational institution that aims to formulate and promote conservative public policies based on the principles of free enterprise, limited government, individual freedom, traditional American values, and a strong national defense. In education polity, the Heritage Foundation supports returning authority to the states and empowering parents with school choice. It publishes numerous reports, including "Common Core Standards' Devastating Impact on Literary Study and Analytical Thinking."

National Alliance for Public Charter Schools
1101 Fifteenth Street NW, Suite 1010, Washington, DC 20005
(202) 289-2700 • fax: (202) 289-4009
e-mail: info@publiccharters.org
website: www.publiccharters.org

The National Alliance for Public Charter Schools is a nonprofit organization committed to advancing the quality, growth, and sustainability of charter schools. The alliance provides assistance to state charter school associations and resource centers, develops and advocates for improved state and federal policies, and serves as the united voice for a large and diverse movement at the state and national levels. It has information about US charter schools at its website.

National Center for Fair and Open Testing (FairTest)
PO Box 300204, Jamaica Plain, MA 02130
(617) 477-9792
website: www.fairtest.org

The National Center for Fair and Open Testing (FairTest) advances quality education and equal opportunity by promoting fair, open, valid, and educationally beneficial evaluations of students, teachers, and schools. FairTest's Assessment Reform Network aims to facilitate the exchange of information and ideas among teachers, parents, and organizations seeking to improve student-assessment practices in their communities. FairTest publishes numerous fact sheets available at its website, including "A Better Way to Evaluate Schools."

National Education Association (NEA)
1201 Sixteenth Street NW, Washington, DC 20036-3290
(202) 833-4000 • fax: (202) 822-7974
website: www.nea.org

The National Education Association (NEA) is an educator membership organization that works to advance the rights of educators and students. The NEA focuses its energy on improving the quality of teaching, increasing student achievement, and making schools safe places to learn. Among the magazines that the NEA publishes are *NEA Today* and *Thought & Action*.

Thomas B. Fordham Institute

1016 Sixteenth Street NW, 8th Floor, Washington, DC 20036
(202) 223-5452
e-mail: thegadfly@edexcellence.net
website: www.edexcellence.net

The Thomas B. Fordham Institute aims to advance educational excellence for every child. The institute promotes education reform through research, analysis, and commentary. It has a wide variety of research available at its website, including the report "What Parents Want: Education Preferences and Trade-offs."

United States Department of Education

400 Maryland Avenue SW, Washington, DC 20202
(800) 872-5327
website: www.ed.gov

The United States Department of Education was established with the goal of improving education nationwide through the use of federally mandated programs. Initiatives by the Department of Education have focused on increasing the accountability of public schools and teachers, as well as providing research and evaluation on school issues. It publishes a variety of newsletters on specific topics related to education, and its National Center for Education Statistics compiles annual information through its National Assessment of Educational Progress (NAEP).

Bibliography of Books

Kathleen Knight Abowitz *Publics for Public Schools: Legitimacy, Democracy, and Leadership*. Boulder, CO: Paradigm Publishers, 2014.

Keen Babbage *Can Schools Survive?: Questions to Ask, Actions to Take*. Lanham, MD: Rowman & Littlefield Education, 2014.

Mary C. Bounds *A Light Shines in Harlem: New York's First Charter School and the Movement It Led*. Chicago, IL: Chicago Review Press, 2014.

Phil Boyle and Del Burns *Preserving the* Public *in Public Schools: Visions, Values, Conflicts, and Choices*. Lanham, MD: Rowman & Littlefield Education, 2012.

Michael Brick *Saving the School: The True Story of a Principal, a Teacher, a Coach, a Bunch of Kids, and a Year in the Crosshairs of Education Reform*. New York: Penguin Press, 2012.

Dave F. Brown *Why America's Public Schools Are the Best Place for Kids: Reality vs. Negative Perceptions*. Lanham, MD: Rowman & Littlefield Education, 2011.

Kristen L. Buras *Charter Schools, Race, and Urban Space: Where the Market Meets Grassroots Resistance*. New York: Routledge, 2014.

Justin Collins	*Burning Cash: How Costly Public School Failures Have Charred the American Dream*. Lanham, MD: Rowman & Littlefield Education, 2014.
Catherine Cornbleth	*Understanding Teacher Education in Contentious Times: Political Cross-Currents and Conflicting Interests*. New York: Routledge, 2013.
Craig S. Engelhardt	*Education Reform: Confronting the Secular Ideal*. Charlotte, NC: Information Age Publishing, 2013.
Michael Fabricant and Michelle Fine	*The Changing Politics of Education: Privatization and the Dispossessed Lives Left Behind*. Boulder, CO: Paradigm Publishers, 2013.
Greg Forster and C. Bradley Thompson, eds.	*Freedom and School Choice in American Education*. New York: Palgrave Macmillan, 2011.
Charles L. Glenn	*Contrasting Models of State and School: A Comparative Historical Study of Parental Choice and State Control*. New York: Continuum, 2011.
Dana Goldstein	*The Teacher Wars: A History of America's Most Embattled Profession*. New York: Doubleday, 2014.
Paul C. Gorski and Kristien Zenkov, eds.	*The Big Lies of School Reform: Finding Better Solutions for the Future of Public Education*. New York: Routledge, 2014.

Steven K. Green	*The Bible, the School, and the Constitution: The Clash That Shaped Modern Church-State Doctrine.* New York: Oxford University Press, 2012.
Jay P. Greene	*Why America Needs School Choice.* New York: Continuum, 2011.
William Hayes	*Consensus: Education Reform Is Possible.* Lanham, MD: Rowman & Littlefield Education, 2013.
Frederick M. Hess and Michael Q. McShane, eds.	*Common Core Meets Education Reform: What It All Means for Politics, Policy, and the Future of Schooling.* New York: Teachers College Press, 2013.
Emile Lester	*Teaching About Religions: A Democratic Approach for Public Schools.* Ann Arbor: University of Michigan Press, 2011.
Christopher A. Lubienski and Sarah Theule Lubienski	*The Public School Advantage: Why Public Schools Outperform Private Schools.* Chicago, IL: University of Chicago Press, 2013.
Warren A. Nord	*Does God Make a Difference? Taking Religion Seriously in Our Schools and Universities.* New York: Oxford University Press, 2010.
Diane Ravitch	*Reign of Error: The Hoax of the Privatization Movement and the Danger to America's Public Schools.* New York: Vintage, 2014.

Nancy Schniedewind and Mara Sapon-Shevin	*Educational Courage: Resisting the Ambush of Public Education*. Boston, MA: Beacon Press, 2012.
Arthur Shapiro	*Education Under Siege: Frauds, Fads, Fantasies, and Fictions in Educational Reform*. Lanham, MD: Rowman & Littlefield Education, 2013.
Alan J. Singer	*Education Flashpoints: Fighting for America's Schools*. New York: Routledge, 2014.
Joel Spring	*American Education*. 16th ed. New York: McGraw-Hill, 2013.
Gail L. Sunderman, ed.	*Charting Reform, Achieving Equity in a Diverse Nation*. Charlotte, NC: Information Age Publishing, 2013.
Paul Tough	*How Children Succeed: Grit, Curiosity, and the Hidden Power of Character*. New York: Houghton Mifflin Harcourt, 2012.
Herbert J. Walberg	*Tests, Testing, and Genuine School Reform*. Stanford, CA: Hoover Institution Press, 2011.
William H. Watkins, ed.	*The Assault on Public Education: Confronting the Politics of Corporate School Reform*. New York: Teachers College Press, 2012.

Index

A

B

C

D

E

F

G

H

I

J

K

L

M

R

S

T

U